Beginning Learner's
Levantine
Arabic
Dictionary

lingualism

© 2020 by Matthew Aldrich

The author's moral rights have been asserted.

All rights reserved. No part of this document may be reproduced or transmitted in any form or by any means, electronic, mechanical, photocopying, recording, or otherwise, without prior written permission of the publisher.

ISBN: 978-1-949650-10-5

Edited by Matthew Aldrich and Nadine-Lama Choucaire

Audio by Nadine-Lama Choucaire

website: www.lingualism.com

email: contact@lingualism.com

Table of Contents

Introduction iii

Using the Dictionary iv

Tips for Looking Up Words vi

Arabic-English Dictionary 1

    ا 1

    ب 13

    ت 22

    ث 30

    ج 31

    ح 35

    خ 42

    د 47

    ذ 51

    ر 52

    ز 57

    س 60

    ش 66

    ص 72

    ض 76

    ط 78

ظ	81
ع	82
غ	89
ف	92
ق	97
ك	102
ل	108
م	113
ن	131
ه	137
و	141
ي	146
English-Arabic Index	148

Introduction

Whether you are a complete newcomer to the Arabic language or have previously studied Modern Standard Arabic or a colloquial dialect, the *Beginning Learner's Levantine Arabic Dictionary* will help you gain a solid foundation in Arabic as it is spoken today. Beyond just being a reference in which to look up words to understand what you hear or express yourself, this dictionary is designed to be a self-study tool which you can explore to build your core vocabulary and understanding of the language through the headwords, translations, grammar and usage notes, example sentences, and free downloadable audio tracks.

Levantine Arabic is an umbrella term that refers to the spoken varieties in the northeastern corner of the Arab world, including Palestine, Jordan, Syria, and Lebanon. As there are small differences in vocabulary, pronunciation, and even grammar from region to region, it is not possible or practical to document and include all of the variations. Instead, for the sake of simplicity and consistency, we have chosen the Beiruti dialect as a basis for this dictionary. This does not imply that Beiruti (Lebanese) Arabic is in any way superior to other regional varieties. That said, you should find it easy to communicate with people throughout the Levant using what you learn in this book. There will be subtle differences, but these you can note, as needed, to hone your style to match a regional variety, if that is your goal.

I would like to thank Nadine-Lama Choucaire for partnering with me on this project to produce a fantastic and much-needed resource for Arabic learners.

FREE ACCOMPANYING AUDIO

You can download or stream the accompanying audio tracks from our website, where you can also find other resources.

www.lingualism.com/BLLAD

Using the Dictionary

To use a dictionary in any language, you need to be somewhat familiar with the writing system and grammar. We assume that you have at least familiarized yourself with the Arabic alphabet, but by no means are you expected to have mastered it. For quick reference, at the beginning of the section for each letter, you can find its pronunciation, various written forms, and its position in the alphabetical order. Remember, of course, that Arabic is written from right to left.

Each entry in the dictionary begins with a **headword** ① in large, bold font followed by its **part of speech** ② and **inflected forms** ③ including irregular plurals, elatives, and imperfect verbs. On the next line, the **English translation** ④ is followed by an **example sentence** ⑤.

Entries, columns, and pages are arranged from left to right (as this is essentially a book *in* English *about* Arabic), but Arabic is written from right to left. So, when an example sentence wraps onto the next line, it continues from the middle of the line, that is, before the English translation starts to its right, as shown with arrows in the above entry.

① ② ③
كبير ADJECTIVE (ELATIVE: أكبر, PLURAL: كبار)
④ big, large ⑤ منعيش بهيداك البيت الكبير عالتلة. We live in that big house on the hill.

- Any relevant notes follow the entry in a gray box. References to entries or notes in other parts of the dictionary are preceded by the symbol ⮕.

We have included dozens of valuable notes about grammar, pronunciation, and usage in the dictionary (in gray boxes, as above). A lot of these apply to more than just the entries they follow. However, instead of grouping them together as extended grammar and pronunciation guides, they have been scattered throughout the dictionary to encourage exploration and so that you can see information alongside relevant examples.

Of course, we cannot explicitly highlight every interesting point of grammar for every headword and example sentence. The intention is to teach you what kind of things to look for in the entries and how to use the example sentences to learn more about the language from observation. The example sentences show how words can be used with other words in sentences. By studying these, you can see if a verb requires a preposition before its object, for instance, or get a better understanding of word order and how it compares to English.

Synonyms usually have parallel example sentences. This was done intentionally so that if you come across two words with the same translation, you know that they are interchangeable. This is important because, otherwise, learners are left with doubt in their minds about how to use new words: "Which one is correct? Can I say it this way, too?"

Notes on **pronunciation** appear at the beginning of the section for each letter of the alphabet, as well as in gray boxes under certain entries, especially in the first section (for alif). Each letter's **phonemic transcription** is also given. It is good to become familiar with these symbols, as we use them occasionally in this dictionary and other Lingualism materials when referencing pronunciation.

Tips for Looking Up Words

Arabic dictionaries can be arranged in one of two ways: alphabetically, or more traditionally, by root (three or four consonants around which words are formed). Determining a word's root is an added challenge for learners, so we have opted for a straightforward **alphabetical arrangement** in this dictionary. This presents another challenge, however, as Arabic words can take prefixes and suffixes.

To find a word's basic form listed in the dictionary, you need to be able to recognize and remove any **prefixes** from a word you encounter and want to look up. (Suffixes pose less of a challenge since they appear at the end of a word.) Some knowledge of Arabic grammar is needed to do this with ease, so it may seem a bit daunting at first but gets easier as you learn more about grammar. In the meantime, here are some common prefixes to watch out for and (following the symbol →) what you should look up instead.

> *Note: This does not mean you should always remove the following letters from the beginning of a word. They may, in fact, be a part of the basic word itself. But if you suspect it is a prefix (from your knowledge of grammar or the context) or can't find it the first time you try to look it up, remove it and look up the word again.*

أ Elative adjectives begin with أ. So, if you are trying to look up أكبر and can't find it under أ, try removing the initial letter and looking at entries around where كبر would be in the dictionary. You'll find كبير (big) has the elative form أكبر (bigger/biggest). أ can also be the first letter of some irregular plurals: أطفال (children) → طفل (child)

إ First-person ('I') singular imperfect prefix: إكتب (I write) → كتب (write)

ال definite article: البيت (the house) → بيت (house)

ب is the prefixed preposition 'in' when on a noun: بالبيت (in the house). On a verb, it is a particle that specifies the present tense: بتحب (you love) → حبّ (love)

ت This can be a conjugated second-person ('you') or third-person feminine singular ('she') imperfect verb: تحب (you love). It can, less commonly, be a particle that is prefixed to an already conjugated imperfect verb: تتحب (so that you may love). Note that measure-V verbs begin with ت that cannot be removed. (⊃See p. 22)

ح marks the future tense: حيعمل (he will do) → عمل (do)

ف so, therefore: فأنا (so I…) → أنا (I)

ع means 'on' or 'to' and with a space before the following word in this book unless it precedes the definite article: عالبحر (to the sea) → بحر (sea). But in practice, whether it is prefixed or not varies from person to person.

ك as: كبوليس (as a police officer) → بوليس

ل on a noun means 'to' or 'for.' On an imperfect verb, it means 'so that' or 'in order to.'

م has many uses. It replaces ب in the first-person plural of bi-imperfect verbs, in which case it is always followed by ن: منحب (we love). It can also be an active or passive participle. Some common participles are listed in the dictionary, but if you're having trouble, remove it to find the verb it is based on. متجوز (married) → تجوز (get married). For another interesting use, ⮕see the last note on p. 117.

ما means 'not,' and we do not prefix it in our materials, although some people do.

ن forms the first-person plural imperfect verb: نكتب (we write)

و means 'and.' It is usually prefixed, but many people write it with a space before the following word: وأنا (and I) = و أنا

ي is the prefix for third-person masculine singular ('he') and third-person plural ('they') conjugations: يكتب (he writes), يكتبوا (they write) → كتب (write)

Also, keep in mind that many nouns (and adjectives) have **irregular plurals** formed by adding vowels between the consonants or even dropping them. Look around to see if you can spot the word you are trying to look up in the parentheses for plural forms: مدن (cities) → مدينة NOUN (PLURAL: مدن)

Tashkeel are the diacritics written above or below letters in Arabic. They show short vowels: (َ *a*, ُ *u*, ِ *i*), the lack of a vowel (ْ as in كتاب *ktēb*), or a doubled consonant (ّ as in إنو *ínnu*). Tashkeel can be disregarded when it comes to alphabetical order. To keep the text from being overly cluttered with tashkeel on every letter, in this book and other Lingualism materials, we do not write them when it would be redundant. Firstly, we consider **fatha** (َ *a*) the default vowel, as it is the most common. If a consonant lacks tashkeel, assume it takes fatha. Secondly, sukuun (ْ) is not written on the final consonant of a word, as a final consonant is not normally followed by a short vowel (unlike in Modern Standard Arabic, which has case endings). Finally, the definite article is written without tashkeel, notably without sukuun: البيت *-lbēt* (Here, we should not assume fatha is pronounced above the unmarked ل.)

As a primarily spoken language, Levantine has **no official spelling rules**. There are popular conventions, but individuals may spell words differently or inconsistently even, sounding them out each time they write them. Common alternatives are sometimes given in entries in case you come across variant spellings that may confuse you. (➲ See, for example, ماذا)

An English-Arabic index can be found after the Arabic-English dictionary to help you find words. Please see the introduction to the index on p. 148.

ا

Alif is the first letter of the Arabic alphabet. It can represent the long vowel ā, but it is also used as a carrier for hamza (ء) and/or short vowels. Because alif has so many roles, we need to take a look at each in more detail. Pronunciation notes can be found in the gray boxes on the following pages.

ا ب ت ث ج ح خ د ذ ر ز س ش ص ض ط ظ ع غ ف ق ك ل م ن ه ة و ي

ا PRONOUN, FEMININE

(possessive) **her** شعرا بني. Her hair is brown.
(object) **her** بيحبا. He loves her.

- When ا is added to a word ending in ي, this suffix pronoun pronounced -ya: خلّي xálli (let!) → خليّا xallíya (let her!). After other vowels, a buffer consonant is inserted: ها -ha: خلّى xálla (he let) → خلاها xalláha (he let her).
- At the end of a word, an alif is pronounced short: ا -a
- ⊃ See ي for a table of all pronoun suffixes.

آب NOUN (NO PLURAL)

August يارا لح تسافر بآب. Yara is traveling in August.

- Alif maddah (آ) represents a long vowel at the beginning of a word.

أبحر VERB (IMPERFECT: يبحر)

sail الشخطورة أبحرت الصبح. The boat sailed in the morning.

- At the beginning of a word, alif with **hamza** (ء) written over it represents the short vowel *a*. We could also write it with **fatha** above it (أ), but in this book, we generally omit fatha, the most common short vowel, to avoid cluttered script. If a consonant is not marked, you can assume it takes fatha (that is, is followed by the short vowel *a*.

أبداً ADVERB

never ما بتتصل أبداً. She never calls.

- Alif with two fatha (اً) appears at the end of some adverbs and is pronounced *-an*. Some people write the two fatha on the preceding consonant: أبدً

1 | Beginning Learner's Levantine Arabic Dictionary

إبرة NOUN (PLURAL: **إبر**)

needle. مش عمر لاقي الإبرة. I can't find the needle.

- Alif with hamza written under it is pronounced *i*. We could write it إ with the short vowel sign **kasra** (ِ), but this would be redundant, so we avoid this in this book.

- Kasra is usually pronounced like in the English word s*i*t, but in Levantine Arabic, at the end of a word, it sounds more like s*e*t. In our phonemic transcription system, kasra is always written *i*, so إبرة is transcribed *íbri*. But keep in mind that the two kasra in this word are pronounced differently.

إبن NOUN (PLURAL: **ولاد**)

son. إبني بالمدرسة. My son is at school.

- Notice that the plural form shown for إبن is actually that of its synonym ولد, as the actual plural of إبن is rarely used in everyday language.

أبيض ADJECTIVE (FEMININE: **بيضا**, PLURAL: **بيض**)

white. شعر جدي أبيض. My grandfather's hair is white.

- Although we generally omit fatha in this book (➲ See note for أبحر on the previous page), we do write it when it appears by the letters ي and و, as these letters can be used as consonants and vowels. (➲ See p. 141 and 146)

إتجاه NOUN

direction. أخد الإتجاه الغلط. He went in the wrong direction.

- Shadda (ّ) represents a double consonant. It is used in Arabic instead of writing a consonant twice: إتجاه *ittijēh*

- Notice that kasra, which is normally written below the line (under a consonant), appears immediately under shadda. (Fatha, in contrast, would appear above it: ّ)

- Alif represents a long vowel sound. In Levantine Arabic, it is pronounced very open, as in the English word m*a*n or pl*a*y (but without the glide to y), which we transcribe as *ē*, in most cases. (➲ See the next note)

إتصال NOUN

(phone) call. الإتصالات بالليل مجانية. Calls at night are free.

- When alif is adjacent to consonants pronounced in the back of the mouth and throat (➲ See note for ص), it is pronounced as in the English word f*a*ther, transcribed *a*. It is not always possible to predict alif's pronunciation in a word, so it is best to mimic what you hear in the audio.

إجا VERB (IMPERFECT: **يجي**)

come. عمي إجا خالي من فرنسا. My uncle

came from France.

أجار NOUN
rent. ما فيو يدفع الأجار هيدا الشهر He can't pay the rent this month.

- When a plural form is not listed for a noun, you can assume that it is regular. For non-human nouns, as this one, the regular plural ending is ات: أجارات (rents)

إجتماعي ADJECTIVE
social المشاكل الإجتماعية بتزيد بالبلاد الفقيرة. Social problems increase in poor countries.

- Sukuun (ْ) is written above a consonant to show that it is not followed by a vowel sound: إجتماعي i*j*timē3i

إجر NOUN, FEMININE (PLURAL: إجرين)
leg. إجريا بيوجعوا بعد الرياضة Her legs hurt after exercise.
foot. إجرين البيبي صغار The baby's feet are small.

إجمال NOUN
generality
بالإجمال ADVERB in general, generally بالإجمال، بحب البسس. I generally love cats.

- Adverbs can be formed in several ways. One is by adding the preposition بـ (in). (➲ See examples on p. 14 and under the entry for سرعة)

أجنبي (PLURAL: أجانب)
ADJECTIVE foreign. خالي عايش ببلد أجنبي. My uncle lives in a foreign country.
NOUN foreigner الأجانب ممنوع يشتغلوا هون. Foreigners are not allowed to work here.

أحد NOUN (PLURAL: إيام الأحد)
Sunday. لازم إشتغل هيدا الأحد. I have to work this Sunday.
الأحد ADVERB on Sunday(s) أوقات بشتغل الأحد. Sometimes I work on Sundays.
الأحد الجايي ADVERB next Sunday يمكن نلعب تنس الأحد الجايي. We might play tennis next Sunday.
كل أحد ADVERB every Sunday بزور جدي كل أحد. I visit my grandpa every Sunday.

- Although a noun in its basic sense, 'Sunday' and other days of the week (and months) are mostly used as adverbs of time expressing *when* something happens.

إحساس NOUN (PLURAL: أحاسيس)
feeling, emotion. خبت أحاسيسا She hid her feelings.

أحسن ELATIVE
better. قياس هيدي التنورة أحسن. The size of this skirt is better.
best. أحسن شي إنك تفل It is best that you leave.

3 | Beginning Learner's Levantine Arabic Dictionary

- **Elatives** are usually listed in the entry for the adjective they are derived from. (➲ See, for example, بارد) But this word is irregular in that it is the de facto elative form for the adjective منيح (good). You can see a few more such examples on the following pages.

أحمر ADJECTIVE (FEMININE) حمرا, PLURAL حمر)
red لبست تنورة حمرا. She wore a red skirt.

إخت NOUN, FEMININE (PLURAL خيات)
sister بتحب إختا. She loves her sister.

إختيار NOUN
choice ما كان إختيار سهل. It wasn't an easy choice.

أخد VERB (IMPERFECT ياخد)
take أخدت المفتاح وراحت. She took the key and left.

آخر (PLURAL أواخر)
NOUN end بيعيشوا بآخر الشارع. They live at the end of the street.
ADJECTIVE, INVARIABLE (+ noun) the last __ آخر مرة شفتو، كان طفل. The last time I saw him, he was a child.

- Although technically an adjective, آخر behaves more like a determiner, preceding the noun it is modifying and not agreeing with it in gender or number. The noun does not take the definite article.

أخضر ADJECTIVE (FEMININE خضرا, PLURAL خضر)
green بشرب شاي أخضر لما إمرض. I drink green tea when I'm sick.

أخوت ADJECTIVE (FEMININE خوتا, PLURAL خوت)
foolish بيكون أخوت إذا بيصدق القصة. He is a fool if he believes this story.

أخير ADJECTIVE
last, final خلصت قراية الصفحات الأخيرة من الكتاب. I finished reading the last pages of the book.

أخيرا ADVERB
finally أخيرا خلصت فروضي! I finally finished my homework!

أداة NOUN (PLURAL أدوات)
tool المطرقة أداة. A hammer is a tool.

- We write a sukuun on **taa marbuuta** (ة) to show that it is pronounced *t*, whereas without it, taa marbuuta is silent.

- The regular plural ending ات is normally not listed in entries, except, as here, when an unpredictable buffer consonant is inserted. That is, in this particular word, it is not simply a matter of adding ات to the singular form.

إذا CONJUNCTION
if إذا الطقس منيح، لح يروح عالبحر. If the weather is good, he will go to the beach.

إذا بتريد please! ساعدني، إذا بتريد
Please, help me!

إربعا NOUN (PLURAL: إيامر الإربعا)
ما بشتغل الإربعا. I don't work on Wednesday. Wednesday.

↪ See note for أحد.

أربعة NUMBER
عدد الجهات بالمربع أربعة. The number of sides on a square is four. four.

↪ See note for تلاتة.

أربعطعش NUMBER
بلش يتصرف غلط عالأربعطعش. He started behaving badly at [the age of] fourteen. fourteen.

↪ See note for طنعش.

أربعين NUMBER
تقابلوا بعد أربعين سنة. They met after forty years. forty.

إرتفاع NOUN
إرتفاع الأسعار فاجأني. The increase in prices surprised me. increase, rise.

الأرجح ADVERB
البيبي عم يبكي عشان الأرجح بدو حليب. The baby is crying because he probably wants milk. probably.

الأردن NOUN (NO PLURAL)
هيدا الرجال ملك الأردن. That man is the king of Jordan. Jordan.

• Damma (ُ) is pronounced as in the English word p**u**t or b**oo**k and is transcribed u.

إرسال NOUN
التلفون مش ماشي لأن ما في إرسال. The telephone is not working because there is no signal. signal.

أرض NOUN, FEMININE (PLURAL: أراضي)
الأرض وسخة. The floor is dirty. floor.
بعد العاصفة، الشجر كانوا عالأرض. After the storm, the trees were on the ground. ground.
شترينا أرض من جيرانا. We bought some land from our neighbors. land.
الأرض بتتحرك متل دائرة حول الشمس. Earth moves in a circle around the sun. Earth.

أرنب NOUN (PLURAL: أرانب)
عندي أرنب أبيض. I have a white rabbit. rabbit.

أزبط ELATIVE (ALSO SPELLED: أظبط)
قياس هيدي التنورة أزبط. The size of this skirt is better. better.
أزبط شي إنك تفل. It is best that you leave. best.

↪ See also أفضل and أحسن.

أزرق ADJECTIVE (FEMININE: زرقا, PLURAL: زرق)
عيونك كتير زرق. Your eyes are so blue! blue.

5 | Beginning Learner's Levantine Arabic Dictionary

أسبوع NOUN (PLURAL: أسابيع)
week بروح عالنادي مرتين بالأسبوع.
I go to the gym twice a week.

إستاذ NOUN (PLURAL: أساتذة)
sir إستاذ، بليز فيك تعطيني إسمك؟ Sir, could you give me your name, please?
(male) teacher الإستاذ بيحب تلاميذو.
The teacher loves his students.

• Although you can make this word feminine by adding ة for a female teacher, معلمة is more commonly used. ⟳ See معلمة)

أسد NOUN (PLURAL: أسود)
lion الأسد ملك الحيوانات. The lion is king of the animals.

أسفل NOUN (NO PLURAL)
bottom, underside أسفل جزمتي وسخ. The bottom of my shoe is dirty.

إسم NOUN (PLURAL: أسامي, أسماء)
name ما بعرف أسامي كل تلاميذي.
I don't know the names of all my students.

أسوأ ELATIVE
worse نتايجي بالمدرسة أسوأ من إختي. My grades at school were worse than my sister's.
worst هيدا أسوأ يوم بحياتي! This is the worst day of my life!

أسود ADJECTIVE (FEMININE: سودا, PLURAL: سود)
black الكلب أسود والبسينة سودا كمان. The dog is black, and the cat is black, too.

أشار VERB (IMPERFECT: يشير)
signal بتسمت لتشير إنا بتوافق. She smiled to signal that she agrees.

أصبع NOUN (PLURAL: أصابيع)
finger المرا عندا خاتم بأصبعا. The woman has a ring on her finger.
toe أصبع إجري. عورت أصبع إجري.
I hurt my toe.

أصفر ADJECTIVE (FEMININE: صفرا, PLURAL: صفر)
yellow الشمس صفرا. The sun is yellow.

إضافي ADJECTIVE
additional, further فيك تعطي معلومات إضافية؟ Can you give me further information?

أضرب ELATIVE
worse نتايجي بالمدرسة أضرب من إختي. My grades at school were worse than my sister's.
worst هيدا أضرب يوم بحياتي! This is the worst day of my life!

أعزب ADJECTIVE (FEMININE: عزبا, PLURAL: عزابة)
single, unmarried هو أعزب. He is single.

أعمى ADJECTIVE (FEMININE: عميا, PLURAL: عميان)
blind عندو كلب ليساعدو لأنو أعمى.

He has a dog to help him because he's blind.

أفضل ELATIVE

better قياس هيدي التنورة أفضل. The size of this skirt is better.
best أفضل شي إنك تفل. It is best that you leave.

أقل ELATIVE

less عمر ينام أقل من قبل. He is sleeping less than before.

أكتر ELATIVE

more الصبيان بيحبوا السيارات أكتر من البنات. Boys like cars more than girls.

- This is the elative form of the adjective/adverb كتير.

أكترية NOUN

majority, most (of) أكترية البوليس رجال. Most police are men.

أكل NOUN

food بحب الأكل الإيطالي. I like Italian food.

أكل VERB (IMPERFECT: ياكل)

eat الصبي أكل تفاحتو. The boy ate his apple.

أكيد ADJECTIVE

certain, sure أنا أكيد إنو الصبح. تطلعت عالساعة. I am certain it is morning. I looked at the clock.

ال PARTICLE

the البيت الكبير أبيض. The big house is white.

- The definite article is a prefix in Arabic. There is no indefinite article (a/an), so بيت alone would mean 'a house.'

- The above example contains two adjectives. كبير is used attributively (as part of the noun phrase), while أبيض is the predicate (➲ See note for أنا). Notice that the attributive adjective agrees with the noun in definiteness taking the definite article while the adjective in the predicate does not.

- There are several rules governing the pronunciation of the definite article:

1. Its basic pronunciation is *il*.

2. The *i* is not pronounced at the beginning of a sentence (البيت - *lbēt*) or after a word ending in a vowel.

3. It is pronounced *li* when prefixed to a word beginning in consonant cluster (الكبير *likbīr*).

4. The *l* is assimilated when added to a word beginning in any of the following consonants: ت ث ج د ذ ر ز س ش ص ض ط ظ ل ن. That is, the *l* is not pronounced (but still written), while the consonant is pronounced doubled: الشمس -*ššámis*.

إلا CONJUNCTION

All كلّ المعازيم فلوا إلا إختي. except the guests left except my sister.

أخ

et cetera, etc., and so on. لح نبلش بأول تمرين، بعدين التاني وأخ. We will start with the first exercise, then the second, etc.

- This is borrowed from the Modern Standard Arabic abbreviation إلخ (إلى آخره). It is pronounced *aláx* in Levantine Arabic.

ألف NUMBER

thousand. الولد الصغير فيه يعدّ للألف. The young boy can count to a thousand.

الله NOUN

God. سألت الله يحميلا ولادا. She asked God to protect her children.

ألماني NOUN, ADJECTIVE (PLURAL: ألمان)

German. هو ألماني. He is German.

إلو PSEUDO-VERB

have. هول الورود إلن ريحة حلوة. Those flowers have a nice smell.

YOU F.	إلك	YOU M.	—
YOU PL.	إلكن	WE	إلنا
	إلك		إلي

SHE	إلا	HE	إلو
		THEY	إلن

ما... إلو (+ perfect tense verb) haven't __ in..., it's been... since. إلي سنة ما شفتا. I haven't seen her in a year.; It's been a year since I saw her.

- A pseudo-verb is a word which is not grammatically a verb but translates as a verb in English. Here, 'have' is expressed by the prepositional phrase إلو (literally 'to him').

his. هيدا الكتاب إلو. This book is his.; هيدا الجزدان إلا. This bag is hers. for. عندي أخبار منيحة إلك. I have good news for you.

إم NOUN, FEMININE

mother, mom. الصبي الصغير باس إمو. The little boy kissed his mom.

- When a plural form is not listed for a noun, you can assume that its plural is regular. For feminine human nouns, as this one, the regular plural ending is ـات: إمات (mothers)

إمتحان NOUN

test, exam. نجح الإمتحان. He passed the examination.

أمل NOUN (PLURAL: أمال)

hope. خطابو عطاني أمل. His speech

gave me hope.

آمن VERB (IMPERFECT: يآمن)

believe. بيآمن بالله He believes in God.

آمن ADJECTIVE

safe. هيدا مكان آمن. This place is safe.

- When an elative form is not listed for an adjective, it can mean one of two things. Either the elative (➲ See note for بارد) is formed by placing أكتر after the adjective (آمن أكتر safe**r**) or the adjective is, logically, never (or rarely) made elative.

أمنية NOUN

wish. عمول أمنية. Make a wish!

أمير NOUN (PLURAL: أمرا)

prince. الأمير ما عندو خي. The prince doesn't have a brother.

أميركا NOUN (NO PLURAL), FEMININE

America. قريبي بيدرس بأميركا. My cousin studies in America.

أنا PRONOUN

(in equational sentence) I am أنا من لبنان. I'm from Lebanon.

(+ verb) I أنا ما بحبو. I don't like it.

- Subject pronouns are not used as much in Arabic as they are in English because conjugated verbs already contain information about the subject. بعيش means 'I live.' Saying أنا بعيش

would be redundant, unless you want to emphasize the subject, as in the second sense above. Subject pronouns are more often used in equational sentences (that is, sentences without a verb), as in the first sense above.

إنت PRONOUN, MASCULINE

you من وين إنت؟ Where are you from?

- Levantine Arabic has three pronouns for 'you.' إنت is masculine singular, which means it is used to address one male person. The feminine singular form is إنتي, while the plural, used for addressing two or more people, is إنتو.

أنتج VERB (IMPERFECT: ينتج)

produce. أنتج الفيلم هيدي السنة. He produced the movie this year.

الإنترنت NOUN (NO PLURAL)

the internet. الإنترنت بطيء بلبنان. The internet is slow in Lebanon.

إنتو PRONOUN, PLURAL

you من وين إنتو؟ Where are you (guys) from?

إنتي PRONOUN, FEMININE

you من وين إنتي؟ Where are you from?

أنثى NOUN, FEMININE (PLURAL: إناث)

female. البسينة ذكر أو أنثى؟ Is the cat male or female?

إنذار NOUN

warning, notice. وصلني إنذار من البوليس. I received a notice from the police.

إنكليزي NOUN (NO PLURAL)

(language) English. الكتاب بالإنكليزي. The book is in English.

- The letter ك is pronounced voiced, as a hard *g* sound (as in the English word *g*as) in this particular word.

آنسة NOUN

miss. آنسة نور معلمتي. Miss Nour is my teacher.

- Titles (Mr., Ms., Miss, etc.) are followed by the person's last name in English. In Arabic, they more often followed by the person's first name, as in the above example.

إنفرادي ADJECTIVE

single. حجزت غرفة إنفرادية. I booked a single room.

إنو CONJUNCTION

that. أنا مأكد إنو لح يتصل قريبا. I'm sure that he'll call soon.; نحنا كتير مبسوطين إنو شفناك. We are very happy to see you.; قالت إنو بتشتغل هون. She said that she works here.

- The ـو ending is a pronoun suffix and can according to the following subject (إنك that you…, etc.), but it can also remain invariable, as can be seen in the example sentences.

أهبل ADJECTIVE (FEMININE: هبلا, PLURAL: هبل)

silly, stupid. هيدي البنت هبلا. This girl is silly.

أهل NOUN (PLURAL: أهالي)

parents. أهلي عايشين حدي. My parents live next to me.

- Although grammatically singular, because this word refers to two people, grammatical agreement is usually plural. In the above example, we see that the active participle عايشين has the plural ending ـين.

أهلا INTERJECTION

welcome. أهلا! قعود هون! Welcome! Sit here!

أو CONJUNCTION

or. بدك دجاج أو سمك؟ Do you want chicken or fish?

أو… أو… either… or…

بدي أو الشوكولا أو الكيك. I want either the chocolate or the cake.

أوتيل NOUN

hotel. الأوتيل أربع نجوم. The hotel is four stars.

أوروبا NOUN (NO PLURAL), FEMININE

Europe. إيطاليا بأوروبا. Italy is in

Europe.

أوضة NOUN (PLURAL: **أوض**)

room. دهنت الأوضة زهر. She painted the room pink.

أوضة قعدة living room. شتريت كنباية لأوضة القعدة. I bought a sofa for the living room.

أوضة نوم bedroom. سارة عم تفتش ع شقة فيا أوضة نوم وحدة. Sarah is looking for an apartment with one bedroom.

- 'Living room' and 'bedroom' are compound nouns, known as **idaafa** constructions in Arabic. When the first word in the construction ends in ة it is pronounced -it, which we write with sukuun (ْ) in this dictionary to remind you of its pronunciation. Normally, ة is pronounced -a or -i.

أوقات ADVERB

sometimes. أوقات بشتغل الأحد. Sometimes I work on Sunday.

أوكي INTERJECTION

okay, all right. أوكي، لح إجي بكرا! Okay, I will come tomorrow!

أول ADJECTIVE (PLURAL: **أولانية**)

first. حيواني الأليف الأول كان بسينة. My first pet was a cat.

best, top. هو التلميذ الأول بالصف. He's the top student in the class.

أي INTERJECTION

yes. أي، بعرف. Yes, I know

- An unwritten fatha followed by ي is transcribed as ē. (➲ See notes for ي on p. 146.)

أي DETERMINER (ALSO: **أيا**)

any. ختار أي لون. Choose any color.

أي حدا anyone, anybody. بيصدق أي حدا. He believes anybody.

أي شي anything, whatever. بدي إحضر أي شي عالتلفزيون. I want to watch whatever on TV.

أي وقت anytime. فيك تزورني أي وقت. You can visit me anytime.

- An unwritten fatha followed by a final ي is transcribed as ayy, but in reality, a final consonant is never pronounced double, so it is essentially ay.

أيا DETERMINER

which. أيا فيلم بدك تحضر؟ Which movie do you want to watch?

أيار NOUN (NO PLURAL)

May. شهر حزيران بعد أيار. The month of June is after May.

إيد NOUN, FEMININE (PLURAL: **إيدين**)

hand. بكتب بإيدي الشمال. I write with my left hand.

arm. عندو علامة ع إيدو. He has a mark on his arm.

11 | Beginning Learner's Levantine Arabic Dictionary

إيطالي ADJECTIVE

Italian. بحبّ الأكل الإيطالي. I love Italian food.

إيطاليا NOUN (NO PLURAL), FEMININE

Italy. هو من إيطاليا. He is from Italy.

أيلول NOUN (NO PLURAL)

September. عيد ميلادي بأيلول. My birthday is in September.

أيمتى ADVERB

when. أيمتى رجعت ع بيروت؟ When did you get back to Beirut?

إيميل NOUN

email. بعتلك إيميل. I sent you an email.

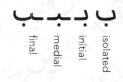

isolated
initial
medial
final

Baa is the second letter of the Arabic alphabet. It is normally pronounced b (as in the word <u>b</u>oy), but it can become unvoiced at the end of a word, sounding like p. It also represents p in foreign words, in which case it may also be written with three dots: پ Phonemic transcription: **b**

ا ب ت ث ج ح خ د ذ ر ز س ش ص ض ط ظ ع غ ف ق ك ل م ن ه و ي

بـ PREPOSITION (ALSO: بـ)

in بعيش بمدينة كبيرة. I live in a big city.

at الولاد بالمدرسة. The children are at school.

- This preposition is prefixed onto the following word. Notice in the first example above that the first بـ is not the preposition but the 1st person singular prefix for bi-imperfect verbs. We see the preposition بـ on the second word.

- A far less common synonym is في, which is mainly used with pronoun suffixes. (➲ See فيو)

باب NOUN (PLURAL: بواب)

door ليش الباب مفتوح؟ Why is the door open?

بابا NOUN (NO PLURAL)

dad بابا شترى سيارة جديدة. My dad bought a new car.

بارد ADJECTIVE (ELATIVE: أبرد)

cold, cool الأكل بارد. The food is cold.

- Short adjectives have elative forms, analogous to comparative (cold**er**) and superlative (cold**est**) forms in English. أبرد (colder), الأبرد (the coldest)

➲ See also note for آمن.

باركينغ NOUN

parking lot الباركينغ مليان سيارات. The parking lot is full of cars.

باس VERB (IMPERFECT: يبوس)

kiss بلبنان منبوس تلات مرات. In Lebanon, we kiss three times.

13 | Beginning Learner's Levantine Arabic Dictionary

- Be careful! There are cultural rules for when and how to kiss on the cheek, when to shake hands, and when to avoid either. ⮕ See the blog article on our website: www.lingualism.com/kiss

باسكت (بول) NOUN (NO PLURAL)

basketball حضرت مباراة باسكت عالتي في. I watched the basketball game on TV.

باص NOUN

bus لوين رايح هيدا الباص؟ Where does this bus go?

باع (يبيع) VERB (IMPERFECT:

sell باع سيارتو. He sold his car.

- In dictionaries, the base form of words are listed. In English, the most basic form of a verb is the infinite. In Arabic, it is the masculine third-person singular verb in the perfect (past) tense. باع literally means 'he sold.'

- The imperfect form has several uses in Arabic, including to build the present and future tenses. By knowing the perfect and imperfect forms, you can conjugate most verbs.

- You can learn more about conjugating verbs in our book *Levantine Arabic Verbs*.

بالتأكيد ADVERB

absolutely فستان العروسة كان بالتأكيد حلو. The bride's dress was absolutely beautiful.

بالظبط ADVERB

exactly الطيارة بتترك بعد بالظبط خمس دقايق. The plane leaves after exactly five minutes.

- Although this word is commonly spelled with ظ, notice that it sounds like ض.

بالفعل ADVERB

quite, really أنا بالفعل تعبان اليوم. I am quite tired today.

بالون NOUN (PLURAL: بلاوين)

balloon كان في كتير بلاوين ملونة بالحفلة. There were a lot of colorful balloons at the party.

باي INTERJECTION

goodbye, bye باي، بشوفك قريبا. Bye! See you soon!

ببلاش ADVERB

(for) free بس تشتري تنين منتج، الأرخص ببلاش. When you buy two products, the cheaper is free.

بتسم (يتسم) VERB (IMPERFECT:

smile بتسم للصورة. He smiled for the photograph.

بحر NOUN (PLURAL: بحور)

sea الجزيرة بنص البحر. The island is in the middle of the sea.

seaside, beach روح عالبحر بحب. I love going to the beach in the summer. بالصيفية.

بخار NOUN (NO PLURAL)
steam. الحمام كان مليان بخار. The bathroom was full of steam.

بخصوص PREPOSITION
about. أنا مبسوط بخصوص النتيجة. I am happy about the results.

بداية NOUN
beginning. قرا الرسالة من البداية. Read the letter from the beginning.

بدل VERB (IMPERFECT: يبدل)
change. بدل تيابو بعد النادي. He changed his clothes after the gym.

بدو PSEUDO-VERB

	I	بدي	WE	بدنا
	YOU M.	بدك	YOU PL.	بدكن
	YOU F.	بدك		
	HE	بدو	THEY	بدن
	SHE	بدا		

want (+noun). بدي قهوة. I want coffee.
want to (+imperfect verb). ما بدي روح لحالي. I don't want to go alone.

need, require. بدا مساعدة. She needs help.; النبات بدن شوية مي. The plants need some water.

بدون PREPOSITION
without. ما في عيش بدونك! I can't live without you!

برا ADVERB
outside. المنظر برا الشباك حلو. The view outside the window is beautiful.
abroad. معظم اللبنانية عايشين برا. Most Lebanese live abroad.

براد NOUN
refrigerator. حطيت الحليب بالبراد. I put the milk in the refrigerator.

برد NOUN (NO PLURAL)
cold, coolness. هول التياب بيحموا من البرد. These clothes protect against the cold.

برد VERB (IMPERFECT: يبرد)
cool, make cold. الهوا لح يبرد الأوضة. The air will cool the room.

بردان ADJECTIVE
cold, cool. بردان، عطيني الجاكيت بليز. I'm cold. Give me the jacket, please.

برم VERB (IMPERFECT: يبرم)
turn. برم ليشوف مين وراه. He turned to see who is behind him.

برنيطة NOUN (PLURAL: برانيط)

hat بتلبس برنيطة ع راسا. She wears a hat on her head.

برودة NOUN (NO PLURAL)

cold, coolness هول التياب بيحموا من البرودة. These clothes protect against the cold.

بري ADJECTIVE

wild ما تلعب مع الحيوانات البرية. Don't play with wild animals.

بريطانيا NOUN (NO PLURAL)

Great Britain بيحكوا إنكليزي ببريطانيا. They speak English in Great Britain.

بس¹ CONJUNCTION

but نبشت منيح بس ما لقيت مفاتيحي. I searched hard but didn't find my keys.

but, rather ما سافر بالسيارة، بس بالترين. He didn't travel by car but by train.

when أكلت العشا بس رجعت عالبيت. I ate dinner when I got home.

بس² ADVERB

only عندي بس ولد واحد. I have only one child.

just, merely تصلت بس تقول مرحبا. I just called to say hello.

بسبب PREPOSITION

because of ما بيحكوا بسبب المشكل. They don't talk because of the problem.

بسة NOUN (PLURAL: بسس)

cat عندي بسة رمادية. I have a gray cat.

بسكوتة NOUN (PLURAL: بسكوت)

cookie بحب آكل بسكوت مع الشاي. I like to eat cookies with tea.

بسمة NOUN

smile عندو دايما بسمة ع وجو. He always has a smile on his face.

بسينة NOUN

cat عندي بسينة رمادية. I have a gray cat.

بشرة NOUN

skin بتهتم ببشرتا. She takes care of her skin.

بضاعة NOUN (PLURAL: بضايع)

product المحل بيبيع بضاعة قديمة. The store sells old products.

merchandise البضاعة الجديدة بتوصل بكرا. The new merchandise arrives tomorrow.

بطأ VERB (IMPERFECT: يبطئ)

slow down السيارة بطئت عالضو الأحمر. The car slowed down at the red light.

بطاطا COLLECTIVE NOUN

potatoes بحب حط بطاطا بالشوربة. I like to put potatoes in the soup.

بطاقة NOUN

card. بدفع بالبطاقة. I'm paying by card.
ticket. بطاقات الحفلة غاليين. The tickets for the concert are expensive.

بطن NOUN (PLURAL: بطون)

stomach. بطني عم توجعني. My stomach hurts.

بطة NOUN

duck. البطة صفرا. The duck is yellow.

بطيء ADJECTIVE (ELATIVE: أبطأ)

slow. بيمشي بسرعة، بس هي بطيئة. He walks fast, but she is slow.

بعت VERB (IMPERFECT: يبعت)

send. بعتلو إيميل. I sent him an email.

بعتذر

I'm sorry. بعتذر إذا وجعتك. I'm sorry if I hurt you.

بعد ADVERB (ALSO: وبعد)

	I		WE
YOU M.	بعدني	YOU PL.	بعدنا
YOU F.	بعدك		بعدكن
HE	بعدك	THEY	
SHE	بعدو		بعدن
	بعدا		

still. الكيك بعدو بالفرن. The cake is still in the oven.
(not) yet. ما خلص فرضو بعد. He didn't finish his homework yet.

بعد PREPOSITION (ALSO: بعد من)

after. رتاحت بعد الشغل. I rested after work.; منرجع من بعد الفاصل. We return after the break.

بعد الضهر afternoon بخلص شغل بعد الضهر. I finish work in the afternoon.

بعد بكرا ADVERB the day after tomorrow. عنا إمتحان بعد بكرا. We have a test the day after tomorrow.

بعد هيك (من) ADVERB after that رحت عالنادي ومن بعد هيك رجعت عالبيت. I went to the gym, and after that, I went back home.

بعد ما CONJUNCTION after غسل إيديك بعد ما تخلص صحنك. Wash your hands after you finish your plate.
in. بشوفك بعد ساعة. I'll see you in an hour.

- Notice that بعد sometimes translates as 'in' in English, as in the last example above, but the meaning is still really just 'after.'

بعدين ADVERB

later. بشوفك بعدين. I will see you later.
then. قريت كتاب، بعدين رحت عالتخت. I read a book then I went to bed.

بعض PRONOUN

each other حبّوا بعض! Love each other!

together, with each other مع بعض بيعيشوا مع بعض. They live together.

بعيد ADJECTIVE (ELATIVE: أبعد, PLURAL: بعاد)

far, distant بدي سافر ع بلاد بعيدة. I want to travel to distant countries.

far from بعيد عن بعيش بعيد عن المدينة. I live far from the city.; خليه بعيد عن حوزة الولاد. Keep it out of the reach of children.

بقر COLLECTIVE NOUN

cows, cattle ما بشرب حليب البقر. I don't drink cow's milk.

بقلب PREPOSITION

inside بحطّ مصرياتي بقلب جيبتي. I put my money inside my pocket.; الريحة المش منيحة دخلت بقلب البيت. The bad smell went into the house.

بقي VERB (IMPERFECT: يبقى)

stay بقينا بفندق جنب البحر. We stayed in a hotel near the sea.

بكرا ADVERB

tomorrow أي يوم بكرا؟ What day is tomorrow?

بكي VERB (IMPERFECT: يبكي)

cry البيبيات بيبكوا بس يجوعوا. Babies cry when they are hungry.

بكير ADVERB (ELATIVE: أبكر)

early منفيق دايمًا بكير. We always get up early.

بلا PREPOSITION

I	بلايي *balāyi*	WE	بلانا
YOU M.	بلاك	YOU PL.	بلاكن
YOU F.	بلاكي		
HE	بلاه	THEY	بلاهن
SHE	بلاها		

without ما فيي عيش بلاك! I can't live without you!

• This word is pronounced with the stress on the first syllable and two short vowels: *bála*, unless it takes a pronoun suffix, in which case the stress shifts and the second syllable is pronounced long: *balā-*, as in the forms in the above table and example sentence.

بلاستيك ADJECTIVE

plastic ما بحب خزن أكل بالبلاستيك. I don't like to store food in plastic.

بلد NOUN (PLURAL: بلاد)

country لبنان بلد صغير. Lebanon is a small country.

بلدة NOUN

town. بعيش ببلدة صغيرة. I live in a small town.

بلش VERB (IMPERFECT: يبلش)

(+ noun or imperfect verb) start, begin. أيمتى بلشت تتعلم عربي؟ When did you start learning Arabic?

- In English, when a verb follows another, it is often infinitive (want to do, try to do, start to do). Levantine Arabic, in contrast puts the second verb into the imperfect tense, so that both verbs are conjugated for the subject. The above example would literally translate "When you-started you-learn Arabic?"

بلغ VERB (IMPERFECT: يبلغ)

notify, report. بلغت البانك عن عنواني الجديد. I notified the bank of my new address.

بلوزة NOUN

blouse. حبيت بلوزتك! جديدة؟ I love your blouse! Is it new?

بليز INTERJECTION (ALSO SPELLED: پليز)

please. بليز، ساعدني! Please, help me!

- Some people may write پ with three dots to show that the pronunciation is *p*, and not *b*.

بناية NOUN

building. البناية جديدة. The building is new.

بنت NOUN, FEMININE (PLURAL: بنات)

girl. البنت لابسة فستان زهر. The girl is wearing a pink dress.
daughter. هيدي بنتي. This is my daughter.

بندورة COLLECTIVE NOUN

tomatoes. ما بحب آكل بندورة. I don't like to eat tomatoes.

بنزين NOUN (NO PLURAL)

gas(oline). السيارة بحاجة لبنزين. The car needs gas.

بنطالون NOUN (PLURAL: بناطلين)

(pair of) pants, trousers. لبس بنطلون أسود. He wore a pair of black pants.

- In English, some words–such as pants and scissors–are always plural, while, in Arabic, they are singular when referring to one pair.

بنك NOUN (PLURAL: بنوك)

bank. نبيل حط مصرياتو بالبنك. Nabil put his money in the bank.

بني ADJECTIVE

brown. عندا عيون بني حلوين. She has beautiful brown eyes.

بنى VERB (IMPERFECT: يبني)

build. لح يبنوا بناية جديدة هون. They're going to build a new building here.

بهار NOUN

pepper. بحبّ زيد بهار للّحمة. I like to add pepper to meat.

بوابة NOUN (PLURAL: بواب)

gate. لح إنطر عالبوابة الزرقا. I will wait at the blue gate.

بواسطة PREPOSITION

via, by means of. بعتت الرسالة بواسطة البريد. I sent the letter by mail.

بوبو NOUN

(eye) pupil. البوبو أسود. The pupil is black.

بوسطة NOUN

bus. لوين رايحة هيدي البوسطة؟ Where does this bus go?

بوليس NOUN

police; police officer. البوليس وقف الشخص المش منيح. The police stopped the bad person.

بي NOUN (PLURAL: بيات)

father, dad. بيي بيشتغل بشركة. My father works in a company.; بيي شترى سيارة جديدة. My dad bought a new car.

- This noun is, of course, masculine, but it takes the plural ending ات, usually reserved for feminine human nouns.

بيانو NOUN

piano. بدو يتعلم بيانو. He wants to learn the piano.

بيبي NOUN

baby. البيبي بيشرب حليب. The baby drinks milk.

بيت NOUN (PLURAL: بيوت)

house. بيتك كتير كبير! Your house is so big!
home. بدي روح عالبيت. I want to go home.

- Notice that ـيـ ē becomes ـيـ ay when a suffix is added to the word: بيت bēt → بيتك báytak

بيتزا NOUN, FEMININE

pizza. أكلت بيتزا عالغدا. I ate pizza for lunch.

بير NOUN (PLURAL: بيار)

well. البير ناشف. The well is dry.

بيرة NOUN (NO PLURAL)

beer. بيحبوا يشربوا بيرة عالبحر. They like to drink beer at the beach.

بيروت NOUN (NO PLURAL)

Beirut. بيعيش ببيروت. He lives in Beirut.

بيسكوي NOUN (PLURAL: بسكوت)

cookie. بحب آكل بيسكوي مع الشاي. I like to eat a cookie with tea.

بيسيكليت NOUN

bicycle, bike بتعرف كيف تسوق بيسيكليت؟ Do you know how to ride a bike?

بيسين NOUN

swimming pool قضيت الصيفية جنب البيسين. I spent the summer by the swimming pool.

بيض COLLECTIVE NOUN

eggs لازم نشتري بيض من المحل. We need to buy eggs at the store.

بيكنيك NOUN

picnic ما رحنا عالبيكنيك بسبب الشتي. We didn't go to the picnic because of the rain.

بين PREPOSITION

(+ pronoun suffix or noun) between البنك بين المطعم والمحل. The bank is between the restaurant and the store.

بين VERB (IMPERFECT: يبين)

seem, appear بين تعبان. He seemed tired.

بينات PREPOSITION

(+ pronoun suffix) between بيناتنا، ما كان الأكل طيب. Between you and me, the food wasn't tasty.

- While the preposition بين can be followed by a pronoun suffix or a noun, بينات is only used with a pronoun suffix.

بينما CONJUNCTION

while دايما بساعد إمي بينما إختي ما بتساعدا. I always help my mom while my sister doesn't help her.

ت تـ ـتـ ـت
isolated / initial / medial / final

Taa is the third letter of the Arabic alphabet. It is pronounced t (as in the word tall). When words that are spelled with the letter ث in Modern Standard Arabic are pronounced as t in Levantine Arabic, they are spelled with ت instead. Phonemic transcription: *t*

ا ب **ت** ث ج ح خ د ذ ر ز س ش ص ض ط ظ ع غ ف ق ك ل م ن ه و ي

تـ PARTICLE (ALSO: لـ)

(+ imperfect verb) **in order to, to, so that** لازم يدرس تيجيب علامات منيحة. He should study to get good grades.

- By imperfect verb, we specifically mean the bare imperfect verb without the prefix بـ.

تابلو NOUN

board. المعلمة كتبت الفرض عالتابلو. The teacher wrote the homework on the board.

تأثير NOUN

effect الموسيقى الرايقة عندا تأثير منيح عالأطفال. Soft music has a good effect on children.

تأخر VERB (IMPERFECT: يتأخر)

be late تأخر البابا ع شغلو. Dad is late for work.

- Notice that there are a lot of verbs on the following pages that start with تـ and have a shadda (ّ) on the second to last consonant. This is a common pattern in Arabic referred to as 'Measure V.' Most (although not) all measure-V verbs are intransitive (that is, do not take an object). You can learn more about verb patterns in our book *Levantine Arabic Verbs*.

- Some people follow write اتـ on measure-V verbs even though the initial *i* is not pronounced in Lebanese Arabic.

تأدب VERB (IMPERFECT: يتأدب)

behave تأدب لمن تحكي مع جدك! Behave when you speak to your grandfather!

تاريخ NOUN (PLURAL: تواريخ)

date ما قرروا تاريخ عرسن بعد. They didn't decide on their wedding

22 | Beginning Learner's Levantine Arabic Dictionary

date yet.
history هيدا البلد عندو تاريخ غني. This country has a rich history.

تاعا VERB (FEMININE: تاعي, PLURAL: تاعوا)
(imperative) **come** تاعا لهون! Come here!

تاكسي NOUN (PLURAL: تكاسي)
taxi خلينا ناخد تاكسي! Let's take a taxi!

تالت ADJECTIVE, NUMBER
third. ربح تالت رتبة He got the third rank.

تاني ADJECTIVE, NUMBER
second. أخد المرتبة التانية He took second place.
other, another بحب إتعلم لغات تانية. I like to learn other languages.
else الولد بدو إمو وما حدا تاني The child wants his mother and no one else.

تأنى VERB (IMPERFECT: يتأنى)
be careful رامز بيتأنى لما يحكي. Ramez is careful when he speaks.

تبعو
one's, his هيدا المقعد تبعك؟ Is this seat yours?; البيت تبعنا قديم. Our house is old.

تبعنا WE	تبعي		–

YOU M.	تبعك	YOU PL.	تبعكن
YOU F.	تبعك		
HE	تبعو	THEY	تبعن
SHE	تبعا		

تجاري ADJECTIVE
commercial, retail, business- فتحت محل تجاري. I opened a retail store.

تجاه PREPOSITION
(as regards) **toward** الأهل عندن مسؤوليات تجاه ولادن. Parents have responsibilities toward their children.

تجربة NOUN (PLURAL: تجارب)
experience. رحلتي كانت تجربة حلوة My trip was a nice experience.

تجوز VERB (IMPERFECT: يتجوز)
marry, get married لح يتجوز هيدا الصيف. He will get married this summer.

تحت
PREPOSITION **under** البسينة نايمة تحت التخت. The cat is sleeping under the bed.
PREPOSITION **downstairs** ماما عم تحضر تلفزيون تحت. Mom is watching TV

downstairs.

تحرّك VERB (IMPERFECT: يتحرّك)
move. القرود بيتحرّكوا بسرعة. Monkeys move fast.

تحطّم VERB (IMPERFECT: يتحطّم)
crash. الطيارة تحطمت. The plane crashed.

تحمّم VERB (IMPERFECT: يتحمّم)
shower, bathe. بيتحمم بعد الرياضة. He showers after exercise.

تخانق VERB (IMPERFECT: يتخانق)
fight. الصبيان عم يتخانقوا. The boys are fighting.

تخبّى VERB (IMPERFECT: يتخبّى)
hide. البسينة تخبت بالخزانة. The cat hid in the closet.

- This verb is **intransitive**—it doesn't take an object. Compare with خبّى.

تخت NOUN (PLURAL: تخوت)
bed. بدي إشتري تخت كبير. I want to buy a big bed.

تخرّج VERB (IMPERFECT: يتخرّج)
graduate. لح تتخرج قريبا من الجامعة. She will soon graduate from college.

تدخين NOUN (NO PLURAL)
smoking. التدخين بيقدر يقتل. Smoking can kill.

تدرّب VERB (IMPERFECT: يتدرّب)
exercise. تدرّب قبل المباراة. He exercised before the game.

تذكّر VERB (IMPERFECT: يتذكّر)
remember. ما بتذكّر إسما. I don't remember her name.

ترأّس VERB (IMPERFECT: يترأّس)
lead. ترأست الفريق. She led the team.

ترقية NOUN
raise. أخد ترقية بالشغل. He got a raise at work.

ترك VERB (IMPERFECT: يترك)
leave. تركت ولادا مع إما. She left her kids with her mother.

تروّق VERB (IMPERFECT: يتروّق)
have breakfast. ما بتروّق الصبح. I don't have breakfast in the morning.

ترويقة NOUN
breakfast. الفندق بيقدم ترويقة بالغرفة. The hotel serves breakfast in the room.

ترين NOUN
train. بدي سافر بالترين. I want to travel by train.

تزوّج VERB (IMPERFECT: يتزوّج)
marry, get married. لح يتزوج هيدا

الصيف. He will get married this summer.

- If you listen closely to the audio, you will hear that the ت in this word sounds more like the voiced consonant د d. This is because the consonant immediately following it, ز z, is also a voiced consonant. This is called assimilation and is a result of naturally spoken language.

تساوى VERB (IMPERFECT: يتساوى)
equal. واحد وواحد بيساوي تنين One and one equals two.

تسبّب بـ VERB (IMPERFECT: يتسبّب)
cause. الشتي تسبب بفيضان The rain caused a flood.

تسبح VERB (IMPERFECT: يتسبح)
swim. فيك تتسبح؟ Can you swim?

تسعة NUMBER
nine. تسعة من رفقاتي ما إجوا عالحفلة Nine of my friends didn't come to the party.

➲ See note for تلاتة.

تسعتعش NUMBER
nineteen. شتريت أول سيارة عالتسعتعش I bought my first car at [the age of] nineteen.

➲ See note for طنعش.

تسعين NUMBER
ninety. بحب إسمع موسيقى من التسعينات I like to listen to music from the '90s.

تسلاية NOUN
fun. بلعب بيانو للتسلاية I play the piano for fun.

تسلّق VERB (IMPERFECT: يتسلّق)
climb. بيحب يتسلق جبال He likes to climb mountains.

تسلّى VERB (IMPERFECT: يتسلّى)
have fun, enjoy oneself. تسليت بالرحلة I had fun on the trip.

تسوّق VERB (IMPERFECT: يتسوّق)
shop, go shopping. بتسوق مع إمي I shop with my mother.

تشرين الأول NOUN (NO PLURAL)
October. لح زور المكان بتشرين الأول I will visit the place in October.

تشرين التاني NOUN (NO PLURAL)
November. تشرين التاني بعد تشرين الأول November is after October.

تشكّى VERB (IMPERFECT: يتشكّى)
report. تشكى عليه للبوليس He reported him to the police.

تصالح VERB (IMPERFECT: يتصالح)
reconcile, make up. تصالحت مع

زَوجا. She reconciled with her husband.

تصرّف VERB (IMPERFECT: يتصرّف)
behave. تصرّف اليوم متل الأطفال He behaved like a child today.

تصل VERB (IMPERFECT: يتصل)
call, phone. تصلت لإعزما I called to invite her.

تطلّع VERB (IMPERFECT: يتطلّع)
look at. تطلّع عالجبل من الشباك He looked at the mountain from the window.

تطوّر VERB (IMPERFECT: يتطوّر)
develop. المدينة تطوّرت مع الوقت. The city developed with time.

تعبان ADJECTIVE
tired. كانت تعبانة بعد ما نضّفت البيت. She was tired after cleaning the house.

تعجّب VERB (IMPERFECT: يتعجّب)
wonder. تعجّب ليه ما تصلت He wondered why she didn't call.

تعشّى VERB (IMPERFECT: يتعشّى)
have dinner. تعشّينا بالمطعم. We had dinner at the restaurant.

تعلّم VERB (IMPERFECT: يتعلّم)
learn. الولاد الصغار بيتعلموا لغات جديدة بسرعة. Small children learn new languages fast.

تعليم NOUN (PLURAL: تعاليم)
education. التعليم كتير منيح بأوروبا. Education is very good in Europe.

تعمّر VERB (IMPERFECT: يتعمّر)
be built. المطار تعمّر السنة الماضية. The airport was built last year.

تغدّى VERB (IMPERFECT: يتغدّى)
have lunch. تغدّى بالشغل He had lunch at work.

تغيّر VERB (IMPERFECT: يتغيّر)
change. الوقت بيتغيّر بالشتوية. The time changes in winter.

تفاح COLLECTIVE NOUN
apples. هبة بتحب تاكل تفاح. Hiba likes to eat apples.

تقريبا ADVERB
around, about, nearly. بعد تقريبا خمس دقايق، وصلت. After nearly five minutes, she arrived.

تقرير NOUN (PLURAL: تقارير)
report. الدكتور كتب تقرير. The doctor wrote a report.

تقيل ADJECTIVE (ELATIVE: أتقل, PLURAL: تقال)
heavy. العلبة كتير تقيلة. The box is very heavy.

تكل ع VERB (IMPERFECT: يتكل)
count on, rely on. البيبي بيتكل ع إمو لتطعميه. The baby relies on his

26 | Beginning Learner's Levantine Arabic Dictionary

mother to feed him.

تلاتة NOUN (PLURAL: التلاتة إيام)

Tuesday. شتغلت التلاتة؟ Did you work on Tuesday?

➲ See note for أحد.

تلاتة NUMBER

three. بدك تلات أو أربع شقف؟ Do you want three or four pieces?

- The ة ending is dropped from the numbers 3-10 before a noun: تلات ـ

تلاتين NUMBER

thirty. لح صير تلاتين قريبا. I'm going to be thirty soon.

تلة NOUN (PLURAL: تلال)

hill. في تلج عالتلة. There is snow on the hill.

تلج NOUN (PLURAL: تلوج)

ice. بيحب يشرب عصير مع تلج. He likes to drink juice with ice. snow. الولاد بيحبوا يلعبوا بالتلج. Kids like to play with snow.

تلطعش NUMBER

thirteen. إبني عمرو تلطعش. My son is thirteen years old.

➲ See note for طنعش.

تلفزيون NOUN

television, TV. ما بحضر تلفزيون الصبح. I don't watch TV in the morning.

تلفن VERB (IMPERFECT: يتلفن)

phone, call. تلفنت لإعزما. I called to invite her.

تلفون NOUN

telephone, phone. تلفوني رن. My phone rang.
cell (ALSO: تلفون محمول) تلفون نقّال phone. نسيت تلفوني المحمول بالبيت. I forgot my cell phone at home.

تلميذ NOUN (PLURAL: تلاميذ)

student, pupil. التلاميذ لازم يسمعوا معلمتن. Students should listen to their teacher.

تم NOUN (PLURAL: تمام)

mouth. خود هيدا الدوا بالتم. Take this medicine orally (lit. by mouth).

تمام ADJECTIVE, INVARIABLE

perfect. الطقس تمام. The weather is perfect.

تمانة NUMBER

eight. الساعة تمانة. It is eight o'clock.

➲ See note for تلاتة.

تمرّن VERB (IMPERFECT: يتمرّن)

exercise. تمرن قبل المباراة. He exercised before the game.
practice. بيتمرن بيانو كل أسبوع. He practices the piano every week.

تَمْرين (PLURAL: تمارين) NOUN

exercise. التمرين كان طويل. The exercise was long.

يتمشكل (IMPERFECT: يتمشكل) VERB

fight. الصبيان عم يتمشكلوا. The boys are fighting.

تمن (PLURAL: أتمان) NOUN

value, cost. تمن هالخاتم كتير مهم. The value of this ring is very important.

تمنطعش NUMBER

eighteen. حط عالكيك تمنتعشر شمعة. He put eighteen candles on the cake.

⮕ See note for طنعش.

تمنّى (IMPERFECT: يتمنّى) VERB

hope. بتمنى شوفك قريبا. I hope to see you soon.
wish. بتمنالك النجاح! I wish you success!

تموز NOUN

July. العطلة الصيفية بتبلش بتموز. The summer vacation starts in July.

تمينين NUMBER

eighty. كلف تمينين دولار. It cost eighty dollars.

تنس NOUN

tennis. بيلعبوا تنس كل سبت. They play tennis every Saturday.

تنضيف NOUN

cleaning. هيدا المحل بحاجة لتنضيف. This place needs cleaning.

تنفّس (IMPERFECT: يتنفّس) VERB

breathe. أوقات بحس ما في إتنفس. Sometimes I feel like I can't breathe.

تنكة (PLURAL: تنك) NOUN

can (container). الأكل يلي بالتنكة مش صحي. Food in a can is not healthy.

تنورة (PLURAL: تنانير) NOUN

skirt. لبست قميص أبيض وتنورة سودا. She wore a white shirt and a black skirt.

تنين (PLURAL: إيام التنين) NOUN

Monday. عندي شغل التنين. I have work on Monday.

⮕ See note for أحد.

تنين NUMBER

two. الرجالين التنين عمومي. The two men are my uncles.

- The word تنين is used for counting, as in one, two, three… It is otherwise only used for emphasis, as in the above example, as the suffix ين alone is usually used to express two of something.

تيناتـ

		(+ pronoun suffix) **both of**
WE	تيناتنا	
YOU PL.	تيناتكن	Both تيناتن مرضا. of them are ill.
THEY	تيناتن	

تهديد NOUN

threat. ما بصدق تهديداتو I don't believe his threats.

تواليت NOUN

bathroom, restroom. ما بيحب يستعمل التواليتات العامة. He doesn't like to use public restrooms.

توقع VERB (IMPERFECT: يتوقع)

expect. توقعت جواب أحسن. I expected a better answer.

تي شيرت NOUN

T-shirt. هيدا تي شيرتي المفضل This is my favorite T-shirt.

تي في NOUN (ALSO SPELLED: تي ڤي)

TV. ما بحضر كتير تي في. I don't watch a lot of TV.

- Some people may write ف with three dots to show that the pronunciation is *v*, and not *f*.

تياب PLURAL NOUN

clothes, clothing. بشتري تياب جداد للعيد. I'm buying new clothes for the holiday.

تيتا NOUN (NO PLURAL), FEMININE

grandma. تيتا، بدك مساعدة بالمطبخ؟ Grandma, do you need help in the kitchen?

تيكت NOUN

ticket. تيكتات الحفلة غاليين. The tickets for the concert are expensive.

 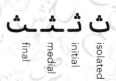

Thaa is the fourth letter of the Arabic alphabet. It is pronounced s (as in the word s̲ix) in Levantine Arabic. It has the same pronunciation as the letter س, but its spelling is retained for words that are spelled with ث in Modern Standard Arabic and pronounced s in Levantine Arabic. Phonemic transcription: **s**

ا ب ت **ث** ج ح خ د ذ ر ز س ش ص ض ط ظ ع غ ف ق ك ل م ن ه و ي

ثابِت (أَثْبَت) ADJECTIVE (ELATIVE:)

fixed, stable. بدفع ع فترات ثابتة. I pay over a fixed period.

ثَبَت (يِثْبَت) VERB (IMPERFECT:)

fix, establish. ثَبَت اللوحة عالحيط. He fixed the painting to the wall.

ثَعلَب (ثَعالِب) NOUN (PLURAL:)

fox. الثعلب بني. The fox is brown.

ثِقة NOUN (NO PLURAL)

trust. عم حط ثقتي فيك. I'm putting my trust in you.

ج

ج ـجـ ـج ـج
isolated / initial / medial / final

Jiim is the fifth letter of the Arabic alphabet. It is pronounced zh (as in the English word vi**si**on or French **j**our). Phonemic transcription: *j*

ا ب ت ث **ج** ح خ د ذ ر ز س ش ص ض ط ظ ع غ ف ق ك ل م ن ه و ي

جامد ADJECTIVE (ELATIVE: أجمد)
The clay المعجون صار جامد. **stiff** became stiff.

جامع NOUN (PLURAL: جوامع)
The أكبر جامع بلبنان ببيروت. **mosque** largest mosque in Lebanon is in Beirut.

جامعة NOUN
university, college أيمتى تخرجت من الجامعة؟ When did you graduate from college?

جاهز ADJECTIVE (ELATIVE: أجهز)
I am أنا جاهز لجاوب عن سؤالك. **ready** ready to answer your question.

جايزة NOUN (PLURAL: جوايز)
He got أخد جايزة أفضل ممثل. **prize** the award for best actor.

جاب VERB (IMPERFECT: يجيب)
receive, get بتجيب دايما علامات منيحة. She always gets good grades.
What are شو لح تجيب عالحفلة؟ **bring** you going to bring to the party?

جار NOUN (PLURAL: جيران)
My جاري عندو جنينة حلوة. **neighbor** neighbor has a nice garden.

جاع VERB (IMPERFECT: يجوع)
be hungry جاع لأن ما أكل من الصبح. He got hungry because he hadn't eaten since morning.

جاكيت NOUN, FEMININE
jacket لازم إشتري جاكيت جديدة للشتوية. I need to buy a new jacket for winter.

---

31 | Beginning Learner's Levantine Arabic Dictionary

جايي ADJECTIVE (ALSO: **جاي**) (FEMININE: **جاية**)
next, coming
فرجيني شغلك الأسبوع الجايي. Show me your work next week.; بتمنى السنة الجاية تكون أسهل. I hope the coming year will be easier.

جبر VERB (IMPERFECT: **يجبر**)
force
الأهل ما لازم يجبروا ولادن ياكلوا. Parents should not force their children to eat.

جبل NOUN (PLURAL: **جبال**)
mountain
الجبل مغطى بالتلج. The mountain is covered with snow.

جبنة NOUN (NO PLURAL)
cheese
باكل جبنة وبشرب شاي الصبح. I eat cheese and drink tea in the morning.

جد NOUN (PLURAL: **جدود**)
grandfather
جدي عندو دقن بيضا. My grandfather has a white beard.

جدو NOUN (NO PLURAL)
grandpa
جدو، فيي إجي معك؟ Grandpa, can I come with you?

جديد ADJECTIVE (ELATIVE: **أجدد**, PLURAL: **جداد**)
new
حضرت فيلم جديد. I watched a new movie.

عن جديد ADVERB (ALSO: **من جديد**) again
إتصل عن جديد. Call again.

جرب VERB (IMPERFECT: **يجرب**)
try, attempt
عم جرب إطبخ أكل لبناني. I'm trying to cook Lebanese food.

جرح NOUN (PLURAL: **جروح**)
cut
عندا جرح على إيدا اليمين. She has a cut on her right hand.

جرح VERB (IMPERFECT: **يجرح**)
hurt, wound, injure
جرحت أصبعي بالسكينة. I hurt my finger with the knife.

جرس NOUN (PLURAL: **جراس**)
bell
رن جرس المدرسة عالساعة تنين. The school bell rang at two o'clock.

• Notice that the verb precedes the subject in this example, which is a common narrative style.

جريء ADJECTIVE (ELATIVE: **أجرأ**)
brave
كانت جريئة بالمقابلة. She was brave in the interview.

جريدة NOUN (PLURAL: **جرايد**)
newspaper
بقرا الجريدة الصبح. I read the newspaper in the morning.

جزء NOUN (PLURAL: **أجزاء**)
part
حضرت أول جزء من الفيلم. I watched the first part of the movie.

جزدان NOUN (PLURAL: **جزادين**)
bag
بيفتشوا الجزادين ع بوابة المركز التجاري. They search the bags at the gate of the commercial center.

جزر COLLECTIVE NOUN (SINGULAR: جزرة)

carrots زرعنا جزر بالجنينة We planted carrots in the garden.

جزمة NOUN (PLURAL: جزم)

(pair of) shoes. نضفت جزمتي. I cleaned my shoes.

فردة جزمة shoe الرجال ضيع فردة جزمتو هو وعم يركض من البوليس. The man lost a shoe while running from the police.

- The word جزمة is grammatically singular but refers to a pair of shoes. The plural form جزم refers to many pairs of shoes, or shoes in general, as in محل جزم (shoe store), while a single shoe is expressed using the word فردة (half of a pair, a single __).

جزيرة NOUN (PLURAL: جزر)

island الجزيرة بنص البحر. The island is in the middle of the sea.

جسر NOUN (PLURAL: جسورة)

bridge في كتير جسورة فوق النهر. There are several bridges over the river.

جسم NOUN (PLURAL: أجسام)

body هو كسر كل عضمة بجسمو. He broke every bone in his body.

- If you listen closely to the audio, you will hear that the ج in the plural form of this word sounds more like the unvoiced consonant š ش. This is because the consonant immediately following it, س s, is also an unvoiced consonant. This is called assimilation and is a result of naturally spoken language.

جعان ADJECTIVE

hungry أنا كتير جعان. I'm very hungry.

جلد NOUN (PLURAL: جلود)

skin بتهتم بجلدا. She takes care of her skin.

جلد VERB (IMPERFECT: يجلد)

freeze جلد الدجاج. He froze the chicken.

جمع VERB (IMPERFECT: يجمع)

collect خالي بيجمع طوابع. My uncle collects stamps.

جمعة NOUN

(PLURAL: جماع) week بروح عالنادي مرتين بالجمعة. I go to the gym twice a week.

(PLURAL: إيام الجمعة) Friday ما بتشتغل الجمعة. She doesn't work on Friday.

⊃ See note for أحد.

- Yes, this word means both 'week' and 'Friday.' You should be able to determine the meaning from the context. You can also use the word أسبوع for 'week.'

جملة NOUN (PLURAL: جمل)

sentence الصبي فيه يكتب جمل صغيرة. The boy can write short sentences.

جنب NOUN (PLURAL: جناب, جوانب)

side الدائرة ما عندا جوانب. A circle doesn't have sides.

جنب PREPOSITION

next to قعد جنبي. He sat next to me.
near بتعيش جنب أهلا. She lives near her parents.

الجنة NOUN

heaven هيدا المكان متل جنة عالأرض. This place is like heaven on earth.

جنس NOUN (NO PLURAL)

sex بياخدوا تعليم جنس بالمدرسة. They take sex education at school.

جنسية NOUN

nationality عندي جنسية وحدة. I have one nationality.

جنوب NOUN (NO PLURAL)

south بعيش بالجنوب. I live in the south.

جنينة NOUN

garden ستي عندا جنينة حلوة. My grandmother has a nice garden.

جهة NOUN

side, direction ضربت الجهة الشمال من سيارتي. I hit the left side of my car.

جهز VERB (IMPERFECT: يجهز)

prepare, make ready جهزت كيك. I prepared a cake.

جواب NOUN (PLURAL: أجوبة)

answer كتب الجواب الصحيح عالورقة. He wrote the correct answer on the paper.

جوز NOUN (PLURAL: جواز)

husband جوزا دكتور. Her husband is a doctor.
pair شتريت جوز صباط. I bought a pair of shoes.

جيبة NOUN (PLURAL: جيوب)

pocket حطيت المصاري بجيبتي. I put the money in my pocket.

جيش NOUN (PLURAL: جيوش)

army الجيش بيحمي البلد. The army protects the country.

- The *l* of the definite article الـ is assimilated before several consonants in Levantine Arabic (➔ See the third note for الـ), including (unlike in MSA) ج. But people tend to pronounce the *l* when the word is at the beginning of the sentence or in careful speech, as in the above example sentence.

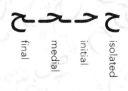

Ḥaa is the sixth letter of the Arabic Alphabet. It is not the same as the English h (which is equivalent to the Arabic letter ه.) It is breathier, as if you are trying to fog up a window. Phonemic transcription: *ḥ*

ا ب ت ث ج **ح** خ د ذ ر ز س ش ص ض ط ظ ع غ ف ق ك ل م ن ه و ي

حاجة NOUN

need حاجة. المي Water is a need. in need of بحاجة لـ أنا بحاجة لمساعدة. I need help.

حاد ADJECTIVE

sharp السكينة حادة. The knife is sharp.

حادث NOUN (PLURAL: حوادث)

accident, incident تأخر لأن كان في حادث ع طريقو. He was late because there was an accident on his way.

حارب VERB (IMPERFECT: يحارب)

fight, battle جدي حارب بالحرب. My grandfather fought during the war.

حاضر ADJECTIVE

present ما كنت حاضر بالعرس. I was not present at the wedding.

حاكم NOUN (PLURAL: حكام)

ruler, governor الحاكم عادل. The ruler is fair.

حالة NOUN (PLURAL: أحوال)

case الحالة صعبة. The case is difficult.

حالو ADVERB

I	حالي	WE	حالنا
YOU M.	حالك	YOU PL.	حالكن
YOU F.	حالك		
HE	حالو	THEY	حالن
SHE	حالا		

35 | Beginning Learner's Levantine Arabic Dictionary

oneself. مهم إنّو الشخص يعرف حالو. It is important that one know oneself.

حاول VERB (IMPERFECT: **يحاول**)
try, attempt. عم حاول إطبخ أكل لبناني. I'm trying to cook Lebanese food.

حب VERB (IMPERFECT: **يحب**)
like. بيحب يقرا كتب. He likes reading books.
love. ستي بتحب بسيناتا. My grandmother loves her cats.

حب NOUN (NO PLURAL)
love. الحب أعمى. Love is blind.

حبس NOUN (PLURAL: **حبوسة**)
prison. البوليس حطو بالحبس. The police put him in prison.

حبلة NOUN (PLURAL: **حبال**)
rope. فيي ساعدك تربط الحبلة. I can help you tie the rope.

حبيب NOUN
حبيبي M. (PLURAL: **حبابي**) **my darling, sweetie**. كيفك حبيبي؟ How are you, darling?
حبيبتي F. (PLURAL: **حبيباتي**) **my darling, sweetie**. تعي لهون، حبيبتي! Come here, darling!

- This word is usually used with the possessive pronoun suffix ي 'my.' We can see the masculine and feminine forms above.

- These terms of endearment are not only used between romantic partners, but also with family and friends. It should not be used with strangers, as it may come off as insincere or even aggressive.

حتوى ع VERB (IMPERFECT: **يحتوي**)
contain. العلبة بتحتوي على صور قديمة. The box contains old photos.

- This verb takes the preposition ع/على before its object.

حجرة NOUN (PLURAL: **حجار**)
stone, rock. الصبي رمى حجرة عالكلب. The boy threw a rock at the dog.

حجز VERB (IMPERFECT: **يحجز**)
book, reserve. حجزت غرفة بالفندق. I booked a room at the hotel.

حد PREPOSITION
next to. قعد حدي. He sat next to me.
alongside, along. إمشي حدي. Walk alongside me.

حدا PRONOUN
someone, somebody. في حدا عالباب. Someone is at the door.
anyone, anybody. بيصدق أي حدا. He believes anybody.
ما حدا no one, nobody. ما حدا بدو حرب. Nobody wants war.

حدعش NUMBER

eleven. الحفلة بتبلش عالحدعش The party starts at 11 (o'clock).

⊃ See note for طنعش.

حدود PLURAL NOUN

border. قطعوا الحدود بالليل They crossed the border at night.

- This noun is always plural in Arabic.

حديد NOUN (PLURAL: حدايد)

iron. المطرقة معمولة من حديد The hammer is made of iron.

حديقة NOUN (PLURAL: حدايق)

(public) park. أخدت ولادي عالحديقة I took my kids to the park.

حديقة حيوانات (PLURAL: حدايق حيوانات)

zoo. شفت فيل بحديقة الحيوانات I saw an elephant in the zoo.

حذر ADVERB

careful لازم تكون حذر بس تقطع الشارع. You should be careful when you cross the street.

حر ADJECTIVE

free ترك الحبس وصار حر. He left prison and became free.

حرارة NOUN

temperature; fever. حرارتو رتفعت His temperature has risen.

حرامي NOUN (NO PLURAL) (PLURAL: حرامية)

criminal, thief الحرامية سرقوا البنك بالليل. The thieves robbed the bank at night.

حرب NOUN, FEMININE (PLURAL: حروب)

war. ترك البلد بسبب الحرب He left the country because of the war.

حرر VERB (IMPERFECT: يحرر)

free, set free. حرر العصفور He set the bird free.

حرف NOUN (PLURAL: أحرف)

letter. في خمس أحرف بإسمي There are five letters in my name.

حرق VERB (IMPERFECT: يحرق)

burn. الشمعة حرقتلو إيدو The candle burned his hand.

- Notice that the verb in the example sentence takes the indirect object لـ (to him), so literally, we have "The candle burned to him his hand."

حرق NOUN (PLURAL: حروق)

burn (wound) حطت دوا ع حرق الصبي. She put some medicine on the boy's burn.

حرك VERB (IMPERFECT: يحرك)

move. حركت الكرسة I moved the chair.

حركة NOUN

movement, move عندو حركات حلوة لما يرقص. He has nice moves when he dances.

حرية NOUN

freedom البلد أخدت حريتا. The country gained its freedom.

حريق NOUN (PLURAL: حرايق)

fire خلّصن من الحريق. He saved them from the fire.

حزيران NOUN (NO PLURAL)

June خلقت بحزيران. I was born in June.

حزين ADJECTIVE (PLURAL: حزانا)

sad قريت قصة كتير حزينة. I read a very sad story.

حسّ حالو VERB (IMPERFECT: يحسّ)

feel حاسس حالو منيح لأن نام منيح. He feels good because he slept well.; بتحسّ حالا وحيدة لما يروح جوزا. She feels lonely when her husband leaves.

- حالو means 'oneself,' so, in Arabic, 'feel' is literally expressed as 'feel oneself.' It's a reflexive construction.

- Notice that the active participle حاسس ('is feeling') is used in the first example above, as it expresses how he is feeling at this moment. In the second example sentence, the bi-imperfect tense is used, as it expresses how she feels in general (every time, not necessarily at this moment).

حسب¹ VERB (IMPERFECT: يحسب)

count, calculate الإستاذ حسب الأجوبة الصحيحة. The teacher counted the correct answers.

حسب² PREPOSITION

according to حسب الأخبار، مزبوط. According to the news, it's true.

حصان NOUN (PLURAL: أحصنة)

horse الحصان عم ياكل جزرة. The horse is eating a carrot.

حصة NOUN (PLURAL: حصص)

portion, share, stake عطينا كل واحد حصتو. We gave each one his share.; (stock) **share** شترى حصص بالشركة. He bought shares in the company.

حصل ع VERB (IMPERFECT: يحصل)

get, obtain حصلت ع دور بالفيلم. She got a role in the movie.

حضّر VERB (IMPERFECT: يحضّر)

prepare, make ready حضّرت كيك. I prepared a cake.

حضر VERB (IMPERFECT: يحضر)

watch حضرت المباراة عالتي في. I watched the game on TV.

38 | Beginning Learner's Levantine Arabic Dictionary

حطّ VERB (IMPERFECT: **يحطّ**)

put, place, set. حطّ الورود عالطاولة. He put the flowers on the table.

حظّ NOUN (PLURAL: **حظوظ**)

luck. بتمنالك حظ منيح. I wish you good luck.

حفلة NOUN

party. الحفلة بتبلش مأخر. The party starts late.
حفلة العيد ميلاد birthday party
حفلة العيد ميلاد بعد الضهر. The birthday party is in the afternoon.

حقّ NOUN (PLURAL: **حقوق**)

cost, amount due. قديش حق هيدا الكتاب؟ How much does that book cost?
right. حقّك ترتاح. It is your right to rest.
correctness, rightness
معك حقّ! معو حقّ be right You're right!
الحق عليه الحق عليّي؟ be wrong Am I wrong?

- Notice the idiomatic expressions above. In English, we use the adjectives 'right' and 'wrong,' as in 'You are right.', while this is literally expressed in Arabic as 'With you is rightness.'

حقيقة NOUN (PLURAL: **حقايق**)

reality, fact. كتشفت الحقايق لحالي. I discovered the facts for myself.
بالحقيقة actually, in reality, as a matter of fact, قالت إنو بتسبح منيح، بس بالحقيقة ما بتعرف. She said that she swims well, but in reality, she doesn't know how to.

حقيقي ADJECTIVE

real. قصة الفيلم حقيقية. The story of the movie is real.

- A 'nisba' adjective is the grammatical term for an adjective formed from a noun by adding ي -i. This word is derived from the noun حقيقة (reality), and because the noun ends in ة, it is first dropped before adding ي. In the above example, we see ة added onto the adjective for another reason: it is feminine in order to agree with the noun it is describing: قصة (story). (➜ See also مركزي)

حكم NOUN (PLURAL: **أحكام**)

(punishment) sentence. ما الحكم كان عادل. The sentence wasn't fair.

حكم VERB (IMPERFECT: **يحكم**)

rule. الملكة بتحكم البلد. The queen rules the country.
sentence. حكموه لسنة بالحبس. They sentenced him to one year in prison.

حكي VERB (IMPERFECT: يحكي)
speak. بيحكي كذا لغة He speaks many languages.
talk. خلينا نحكي عنو! Let's talk about it!

حكي NOUN (PLURAL: حكايات)
speech, talking. الولد الصغير عندو مشاكل بالحكي The little boy has speech problems.

حكيم NOUN (PLURAL: حكما)
doctor. لازم تشوف حكيم You should see a doctor.

حلم[1] VERB (IMPERFECT: يحلم)
dream. بتحلم تصير مشهورة She dreams of becoming famous.

حلم[2] NOUN (PLURAL: أحلام)
dream. عن شو كان حلمك؟ What was your dream about?

حلو ADJECTIVE (ELATIVE: أحلى, PLURAL: حلوين)
beautiful, pretty. هي مرا حلوة She's a pretty woman.
nice, beautiful. الطقس حلو اليوم The weather is nice today.
sweet. هيدا الكيك كتير حلو This cake is very sweet.

حليب NOUN
milk. الطفل بيشرب حليب الصبح The child drinks milk in the morning.

حماسي ADJECTIVE
exciting. المباراة كانت حماسية The game was exciting.

حمام NOUN
bathroom, restroom. ما بيحب يستعمل الحمامات العامة He doesn't like to use public restrooms.

حمل VERB (IMPERFECT: يحمل)
hold. الإم حملت البيبي The mother held the baby.
carry. حملت الإم إبنا عالتخت The mother carried her son to the bed.

حمى VERB (IMPERFECT: يحمي)
protect. البوليس حموا البيت The police protected the house.

حوالي ADVERB
around, about, approximately. بعد حوالي خمس دقايق، وصلت After about five minutes, she arrived.

حوالي PREPOSITION
around, about. كان هونيك حوالي الساعة أربعة He was there around four o'clock.

حوزة NOUN
reach, possession. خلي الأدوية بعيد عن حوزة الأطفال Keep medications out of the reach of children.

حَوْل PREPOSITION

around قعدوا حول الطاولة. Sit around the table.

حَيّ NOUN (PLURAL: أَحْياء)

neighborhood بعيش بحي رايق. I live in a quiet neighborhood.

حَياة NOUN, FEMININE

life ستمتع بحياتك! Enjoy your life!

- Notice that the final ة is pronounced *t*. In this dictionary, we write a sukuun (ْ) over the ة to show this.

حيط NOUN (PLURAL: حيطان)

wall المعلمة قاصصت التلميذ عالحيط. The teacher punished the student [by making him stand] against the wall.

حيلا DETERMINER

any ختار حيلا لون. Choose any color.

حيلا حدا anyone بيصدق حيلا حدا. He believes anyone.

حيلا شي anything بدي إحضر حيلا شي عالتلفزيون. I want to watch anything on TV.

حيلا وقت anytime فيك تزورني حيلا وقت. You can visit me anytime.

حيوان NOUN

animal هيدا الحيوان خطير. This animal is dangerous.

حيوان أليف pet ما عندي حيوان أليف. I don't have a pet.

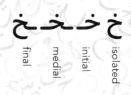

Khaa is the seventh letter of the Arabic alphabet. It is a voiceless guttural sound with no equivalent in English—something between a raspy k and h. It is pronounced like the ch in the Scottish word lo<u>ch</u> or German do<u>ch</u>. Phonemic transcription: *x*

ا ب ت ث ج ح **خ** د ذ ر ز س ش ص ض ط ظ ع غ ف ق ك ل م ن ه و ي

خاتم NOUN (PLURAL: خواتم)
ring شتريت خاتم غالي. I bought an expensive ring.

خاص ADJECTIVE
private الممثل ما بيحب يحكي عن حياتو الخاصة. The actor doesn't like to talk about his private life.
own عندي أوضة خاصة فيي. I have my own bedroom.

خاف من VERB (IMPERFECT: يخاف)
be afraid of, fear أكترية الأطفال بيخافوا من العتمة. Most children are afraid of the dark.

خال NOUN (PLURAL: خوال)
(maternal) uncle خالي عايش بأميركا. My uncle lives in America.

خالة NOUN
(maternal) aunt ميرنا بتحب خالتا. Mirna loves her aunt.

خالتو NOUN (NO PLURAL), FEMININE
(maternal) auntie خالتو، نامي عنا اليوم. Auntie, sleep at our house today!

خايف ADJECTIVE
afraid, fearful
afraid of خايف من الولد خايف من العتمة. The child is afraid of the dark.

خبر NOUN (PLURAL: أخبار)
piece of news نفعل بس سمع الخبر. He got excited when he heard the news.
the news الأخبار PLURAL NOUN الأخبار بتبلش عالتمانة. The news starts at eight o'clock.

42 | Beginning Learner's Levantine Arabic Dictionary

خبز NOUN

bread. أكلت كتير خبز. I ate too much bread!

خبزة NOUN

piece of bread. بحب آكل شقفة خبزة مع الشوربة. I like to eat a piece of bread with soup.

خبط (IMPERFECT: يخبط) VERB

hit. السيارة خبطت الشجرة. The car hit the tree.

خبط (IMPERFECT: يخبط) VERB

knock. خبطت عالباب تلات مرات. I knocked on the door three times.

خبى (IMPERFECT: يخبي) VERB

hide. خبت الكتاب ورا خزانة الكتب. She hid the book behind the bookcase.

- This verb is **transitive**—it takes an object. Compare with تخبى.

ختار (IMPERFECT: يختار) VERB

choose, select, pick. ختار هدية لمرتو. He chose a gift for his wife.

ختـرع (IMPERFECT: يخترع) VERB

invent. الكمبيوتر كان كتير كبير لمن خترعوه. The computer was very big when they invented it.

ختم (IMPERFECT: يختم) VERB

stamp. ختمت الرسالة. She stamped the letter.

ختيار (PLURAL: ختيارية) ADJECTIVE

old. الرجال الختيار بيلبس عوينات. The old man wears glasses.

ختيـر (IMPERFECT: يختيـر) VERB

grow old, age. بتصير الذاكرة ضعيفة بس الواحد يختيـر. One's memory becomes weak as one ages.

خد (PLURAL: خدود) NOUN

cheek. خيي عندو علامة ع خدو اليمين. My brother has a mark on his right cheek.

خدع (IMPERFECT: يخدع) VERB

deceive, fool. ما تخلي حدا يخدعك. Don't let anybody fool you.

خدم (IMPERFECT: يخدم) VERB

serve. الباص بيخدم مدينة وحدة. The bus serves one city.

خرب (IMPERFECT: يخرب) VERB

destroy, damage. خربت العاصفة الزرع. The storm destroyed the plants.

خروف (PLURAL: خواريف) NOUN

sheep. عديت الخواريف. I counted the sheep.

خريطة (PLURAL: خرايط) NOUN

map. بدي خريطة للاقي البيت. I want a map to find the house.

خريف NOUN

autumn, fall وراق الشجر بيوقعوا بالخريف. Leaves fall in autumn.

خزانة NOUN

closet, wardrobe حطيت تيابي بالخزانة. I put my clothes in the closet.

cupboard البهارات بالخزانة. The peppers are in the cupboard.

خزانة كتب bookcase ليش ما في ولا كتاب بخزانة الكتب؟ Why aren't there any books in the bookcase?

خزّن VERB (IMPERFECT: يخزّن)

store خزن أكل لبعدين. He stored food for later.

خزنة NOUN

safe بتخبي الدهب بالخزنة. She hides gold in a safe.

خسر VERB (IMPERFECT: يخسر)

lose خسر شغلو. He lost his job.

خضّ VERB (IMPERFECT: يخضّ)

shake خضّ الدوا منيح. Shake the medicine well.

خضرة COLLECTIVE NOUN (PLURAL: خضار)

vegetables بنتي ما بتاكل خضرة. My daughter won't eat vegetables.

خط NOUN (PLURAL: خطوط)

handwriting خطك كتير حلو. Your handwriting is very nice.

line حط خط تحت الكلمة. Put a line under the word.

phone line الخط مشغول. The line is busy.

خطأ NOUN (PLURAL: أخطاء)

mistake تعلّم من أخطاءو. He learned from his mistakes.

خطاب NOUN

speech عطت خطاب بعرسا. She gave a speech at her wedding.

خطوة NOUN

step أخد خطوة بإتجاه الباب. He took a step toward the door.

خطيب NOUN (PLURAL: خطاب)

(male) fiancé قابلت خطيبا بالجامعة. She met her fiancé at university.

خطيبة NOUN

(female) fiancée بعرف خطيبتو من المدرسة. I know his fiancée from school.

خطير ADJECTIVE (ALSO: خطر) (ELATIVE: أخطر)

dangerous هيدا الحيوان مش خطير. That animal isn't dangerous.

خفض VERB (IMPERFECT: يخفض)

lower, decrease المحل خفض أسعارو. The store lowered its prices.

خفف VERB (IMPERFECT: يخفف)

slow down, go slowly عم بتسوق

بسرعة، خفف! You're driving fast! Slow down!
decrease. المحل خفف سعر المنتجات. The store decreased the price of the products.

خلّص VERB (IMPERFECT: **يخلّص**)

complete, finish. خلّصت دراستا She completed her studies.; خلّص فرضو. He finished his homework.
save. الدكتور خلّص حياتي. The doctor saved my life.

خلص VERB (IMPERFECT: **يخلص**)

end, stop. الحرب خلصت. The war ended.

خلطة NOUN

mix. بستعمل خلطة خضرة لهيدا الصحن. I use a mix of vegetables for this dish.

خلق VERB (IMPERFECT: **يخلق**)

be born. بنت ندى خلقت بالعيد. Nada's daughter was born on the holiday.

خلّى VERB (IMPERFECT: **يخلّي**)

keep. خلت كل الرسايل يلي بعتن. She kept all the letters he sent.
make, cause. خلاها تبكي. He made her cry.
let, allow. خلي لولادو يحضروا هيدا الفيلم. He allowed his children to watch this movie.

خمسة NUMBER

five. عندي خمس بسينات. I have five cats.

➲ See note for ثلاثة.

خمسطعش NUMBER

fifteen. في خمستعشر تلميذ. There are fifteen students.

➲ See note for طنعش.

خمسين NUMBER

fifty. المزرعة فيا خمسين دجاجة. The farm has fifty chickens.

خميس NOUN (PLURAL: **إيام الخميس**)

Thursday. بشوفك الخميس! I'll see you on Thursday!

➲ See note for أحد.

خنزير NOUN (PLURAL: **خنازير**)

pig. الولاد قروا قصة التلات خنازير. The kids read the story of the three pigs.

خوف NOUN (NO PLURAL)

fear. ما قال شي من الخوف إنو يجرحا. He said nothing for fear of hurting her.

خوّف VERB (IMPERFECT: **يخوّف**)

frighten, scare. الخيال خوف الصبي. The shadow scared the boy.

خي NOUN (PLURAL: **إخوة**)

brother. عندي خي وإختين. I have one brother and two sisters.

خِيار NOUN

selection, choice في خِيارات تْياب كْبيرة بالمحلّ. There is a wide selection of clothes in the store.

- A short vowel (**schwa** (ə)–as in the English word pock<u>e</u>t) is–subconsciously for native speakers–inserted between words when a word ends in a consonant and the next word begins with a consonant cluster. The above example sentence offers two examples of this: …*xayārātᵊ tyēbᵊ kbīra*… Listen for this in other example sentences in this dictionary, including in the very next entry.

خْيال NOUN

shadow. شِفْت خْيالك I saw your shadow.

خيفان ADJECTIVE

afraid. ربيع خيفان إنو بيو يقاصصو Rabih is afraid that his father will punish him.

- In the above example, we have the given name ربيع Rabih, which is the word 'Spring' in Arabic. Keep in mind that many given names in Arabic are taken from common words. So, if you see a sentence that seems nonsensical, such as "Spring is afraid…," it might actually just be someone's name.

د د د د isolated / initial / medial / final

Daal is the eighth letter of the Arabic alphabet. It is normally pronounced d (as in the word d<u>o</u>g), but it can become unvoiced at the end of a word, sounding like t. Phonemic transcription: **d**

ا ب ت ث ج ح خ **د** ذ ر ز س ش ص ض ط ظ ع غ ف ق ك ل م ن ه و ي

دائرة NOUN (PLURAL: دوائر)

circle ما بقدر إرسم دائرة منيح. I can't draw a circle well.

department, office راحت ع دايرة البوليس. She went to the police department.

دار VERB (IMPERFECT: يدور)

circle, go around الأرض بتدور حول الشمس. The Earth goes around the Sun.

دافي ADJECTIVE (ELATIVE: أدفا)

warm المكان كان دافي. The place was warm.

داق VERB (IMPERFECT: يدوق)

taste دوق الشوربة. طيبة! Taste the soup. It's delicious!

دايما ADVERB

always بروح دايما ع مطعم منير. I always go to Munir restaurant.

often بروح عالسينما دايما. I often go to the cinema.

دب NOUN (PLURAL: دبب)

bear الدب حيوان تقيل. The bear is a heavy animal.

دبان COLLECTIVE NOUN

flies في كتير دبان حول الزبالة. There are many flies around the garbage.

- Remember that collective nouns can refer to a single individual/item by adding ة. So, 'a fly' would be دبانة.

دبوس NOUN (PLURAL: دبابيس)

pin في دبوس بشعرها. There is a pin in her hair.

47 | Beginning Learner's Levantine Arabic Dictionary

دَجاج COLLECTIVE NOUN (SINGULAR: **دَجاجة**)
chickens, hens دجاجتي بتعطي بيضة وحدة كل يوم. My chicken gives one egg every day.
بدك دجاج أو سمك؟ chicken (meat)
Do you want chicken or fish?

- Notice in the first example above that the singular form **دَجاجة** is used because we are referring to one animal. But when we refer to an animal's meat, we always use the collective form. as in the second example.

دَجَم NOUN
gym. بيرفع أوزان بالدجم He lifts weights in the gym.

دجينز NOUN
jeans. بيلبس دايما دجينز مع قميص He always wears jeans with a shirt.

دُخان NOUN
smoke. بكره ريحة الدخان I hate the smell of smoke.

دَخَل VERB (IMPERFECT: **يِدخُل**)
enter. فتحت الباب لإدخل عالبيت I opened the door to enter the room.

دَخَّن VERB (IMPERFECT: **يِدخِّن**)
smoke. ما بدخن. I don't smoke.

دراسة NOUN
studies, studying بدا تخلص دراستا برا. She wants to finish her studies abroad.

ذُرة NOUN (NO PLURAL)
corn. بيزرعوا ذرة بالمزرعة They grow corn on the farm.

درجة NOUN
step. هين. في بس تلات درجات It's easy. There are only three steps.

دَرَس VERB (IMPERFECT: **يِدرُس**)
study. عم يدرسوا هندسة They are studying engineering.

درس NOUN (PLURAL: **دروس**)
lesson. تعلمت درس من أخطائي I learned a lesson from my mistakes.

دَرَك NOUN (NO PLURAL)
police. الدرك وقف الشخص المش منيح. The police stopped the bad person.

- **درك** is grammatically singular but refers to police (in a collective sense), while **دركي** is a police officer. (➔ See **دركي**)

دركي NOUN (NO PLURAL)
police officer, cop الدركي وقفني لأن كنت عم سوق بسرعة. The police officer pulled me over because I was speeding.

- Instead of using a plural form of this word, **درك** is usually used. (➔ See **درك**)

دعس VERB (IMPERFECT: يدعس)
ما تدعس عالبسينة! Don't step step on the cat!

دفش VERB (IMPERFECT: يدفش)
الصبي دفش إختو. The boy push pushed his sister.

دفع VERB (IMPERFECT: يدفع)
فيك تدفع بعدين. You can pay pay later.

دق VERB (IMPERFECT: يدق)
ا دقيت عالباب تلات مرات. knock knocked on the door three times.
دق المسمار بالخشب. He hammer hammered the nail into the wood.
دقيت لإعزما. I called to call, phone invite her.

دقر VERB (IMPERFECT: يدقر)
ما تدقر وجك! Don't touch touch your face!

دقن NOUN (PLURAL: دقون)
تغير شكلو بس شال دقنو. His beard look changed when he removed his beard.

دقيقة NOUN (PLURAL: دقايق)
الفيلم بلش من خمس دقايق. minute The movie started five minutes ago.

دكتور NOUN (PLURAL: دكاترة)
لازم تشوف دكتور. You doctor should see a doctor.

- In the dictionary, we may only show masculine nouns that refer to jobs or nationalities when the feminine equivalent is formed by adding ة. A doctor who happens to be female would necessarily be دكتورة in Arabic.

- When referring to a nonspecific person, as in the example, the masculine form would be used.

دكر NOUN (PLURAL: دكورة)
الكلب دكر أو أنثى؟ Is the dog male male or female?

دل VERB (IMPERFECT: يدل)
هو لح يدلك ع مقعدك. lead, guide He will show you to your seat.

دلع NOUN (PLURAL: أسامي دلع)
سوسو دلعي. إسمي الحقيقي nickname سحر. Sousou is my nickname. My real name is Sahar.

دليل NOUN (PLURAL: دلايل)
البوليس لقى evidence, clue, lead الدلايل. The police found the leads.

دم NOUN (PLURAL: إدمية)
كان في دم ع وجو. There was blood blood on his face.

دمر VERB (IMPERFECT: يدمر)
العاصفة دمرت الزرع. The destroy storm destroyed the plants.

49 | Beginning Learner's Levantine Arabic Dictionary

دمع COLLECTIVE NOUN (SINGULAR: دمعة, PLURAL: دموع)

tears (eye) كان في دمع بعيونا لمن ودّعتنا. There were tears in her eyes when she said goodbye to us.

دنب NOUN (PLURAL: دناب)

tail البسينات عندن دنب. Cats have tails.

دهب NOUN (NO PLURAL)

gold الدهب غالي. Gold is expensive.

دهن VERB (IMPERFECT: يدهن)

paint دهن الحيط أبيض. He painted the wall white.
spread بدهن أوقات شوكولاتا ع خبزتي. I sometimes spread chocolate on my bread.

دهن NOUN (PLURAL: دهون)

fat الأكل يلي فيه دهن مش صحي. Food that has fat in it is not healthy.

دوا NOUN (PLURAL: أدوية)

medicine هيدا الدوا بيشيل الوجع. This medicine relieves pain.

دوبل VERB (IMPERFECT: يدوبل)

double دوبل أرباحو. He doubled his gains.

دور NOUN (PLURAL: أدوار)

role الممثل لعب دور صعب. The actor played a difficult role.
turn دور مين؟ Whose turn is it?

دور VERB (IMPERFECT: يدور)

search دوّرت منيح بس ما لقيت مفاتيحي. I searched hard but didn't find my keys.

دولاب NOUN (PLURAL: دواليب)

wheel, tire شتريت أربع دواليب للسيارة. I bought four tires for the car.

دولار NOUN

dollar لح أعطيك عشرة دولار. I'll give you ten dollars.

دينة NOUN (PLURAL: دينين)

ear في عندي وجع بالدينة. I have pain in my ear.

ذ ذ ذ
final | medial | initial | isolated

Dhaal is the ninth letter of the Arabic alphabet. It is pronounced z (as in zoo) in Levantine Arabic. It has the same pronunciation as the letter ز, but its spelling is retained for words that are spelled with the letter ذ in Modern Standard Arabic and pronounced z in Levantine Arabic. Phonemic transcription: **z**

ا ب ت ث ج ح خ د **ذ** ر ز س ش ص ض ط ظ ع غ ف ق ك ل م ن ه و ي

ذات الـ

the same ___ سألتني ذات السؤال مرة تانية. You asked me the same question again.

ذاكرة NOUN

memory. ستي عندا ذاكرة قوية My grandma has a strong memory.

ذكر VERB (IMPERFECT: يذكر)

mention. ما ذكرت عمرا She didn't mention her age.

ذكر VERB (IMPERFECT: يذكر)

remind. ذكرني جيب الكتاب بكرا Remind me to bring the book tomorrow.

ذكي ADJECTIVE (ELATIVE: أذكى, PLURAL: أذكيا, ذكايا)

clever, sharp. السعدان حيوان ذكي The monkey is a clever animal.

ر ـر ـر ر
isolated
initial
medial
final

Raa is the tenth letter of the Arabic alphabet. It is not the same as the English r. It is a tap/flap/trill sound (made with brief contact against the roof of the mouth) as in languages such as Portuguese, Scottish, Spanish, Japanese, and Korean. Phonemic transcription: *r*

ا ب ت ث ج ح خ د ذ **ر** ز س ش ص ض ط ظ ع غ ف ق ك ل م ن ه و ي

راح VERB (IMPERFECT: يروح)
go بروح عالسوبر ماركت مرة بالأسبوع. I go to the supermarket once a week. **leave** لازم روح بكير. I should leave early.

راحة NOUN (NO PLURAL)
rest أنا بحاجة للراحة بعد هيدا اليوم الطويل. I need to rest after this long day.

راديو NOUN
radio بتسمع راديو بالسيارة. She listens to the radio in the car.

راس NOUN (PLURAL: روس)
head راسي عم يوجعني. My head is hurting me.

راضي ADJECTIVE
pleased, content معلمتي كانت كتير راضية عن شغلي. My teacher was very pleased with my work.

راقي ADJECTIVE (ELATIVE: أرقى)
classy, fancy, refined, high-class المطعم راقي. This restaurant is fancy.

رئيسي ADJECTIVE
main عنواني الرئيسي ببيروت. My main address is in Beirut.

رايق ADJECTIVE (ELATIVE: أروق)
quiet, tranquil, calm, soft بحب إقرا بمكان رايق. I like to read in a quiet place.; بتحب الموسيقى الرايقة. She likes soft music.

رب NOUN (PLURAL: ربوب)
lord هو رب القصر. He is lord of the castle. **Lord, God** يا رب، ساعدني! Help me, o Lord!

52 | Beginning Learner's Levantine Arabic Dictionary

ربح[1] (IMPERFECT: **يربح**) VERB
win. ربحوا مباراة الفوتبول. They won the soccer game.

ربح[2] (PLURAL: **أرباح**) NOUN
profit, gain. ربح الشركة زاد. The company's profit increased.

ربط (IMPERFECT: **يربط**) VERB
tie. البنت ربطت شعرا. The girl tied back her hair.

ربطة NOUN
necktie. دايما بيلبس ربطة مع قميص. He always wears a tie with a shirt.

ربورتاج NOUN
report. شفت الربورتاج عالتلفزيون. I saw the report on television.

ربيع NOUN (NO PLURAL)
spring. الربيع بيجي بعد الشتوية. Spring comes after winter.

رتاح (IMPERFECT: **يرتاح**) VERB
rest. رتاح بعد الشغل. He rested after work.

رتب (IMPERFECT: **يرتب**) VERB
organize, put in order, tidy up. رتب أوضتو. He tidied up his bedroom.

رتبة (PLURAL: **رتب**) NOUN
rank, position. رتبتو بالجيش عالية. His rank in the military is high.

- Compare the entry word رتبة *rítbi* with its form in the example sentence (رتبتو *rítibtu*). This is a good example of how a word's vowel pattern can change when a suffix is added in Levantine Arabic.

رتفع (IMPERFECT: **يرتفع**) VERB
rise, increase. الحرارة بترتفع بالصيف. The temperature rises in summer.

رجال (PLURAL: **رجال**) NOUN
man. هيدا الرجال لح يصير بي. This man will become a father.

رجع (IMPERFECT: **يرجع**) VERB
return, go back, come back. رجع من الشغل بعد الضهر. He returned from work in the afternoon.
(+ perfect verb) **and then**. قريت كتاب، رجعت رحت عالتخت. I read a book, and then I went to bed.

رجعة NOUN
return. بنتطر بالبيت رجعة ولادي من المدرسة. I wait at home for the return of my kids from school.

رجف (IMPERFECT: **يرجف**) VERB
shake. رجف لأن الطقس بارد. He was shaking because the weather is cold.

رح PARTICLE (ALSO: **لح**)
(+ imperfect verb) **will**. رح إحكيك بعدين. I will talk to you later.

53 | Beginning Learner's Levantine Arabic Dictionary

رحلة NOUN
trip, journey هيدي أول رحلة إلي برّا.
This is my first trip abroad.

رخيص ADJECTIVE (ELATIVE: أرخص, PLURAL: رخاص)
cheap الرحلة كانت رخيصة.; The trip was cheap.; الفضة أرخص من الدهب.
Silver is cheaper than gold.

رد[1] VERB (IMPERFECT: يرد)
reply بعتلا إيميل بس ما ردت. I sent her an email, but she didn't reply.

رد[2] NOUN (PLURAL: ردود)
reply, response الرد كان كتير طويل.
The reply was very long.

رز NOUN (NO PLURAL)
rice بكم بلد بيرموا رز بالأعراس. In some countries, they throw rice at weddings.

رسالة NOUN (PLURAL: رسايل)
letter, message كتبتلو رسالة طويلة.
I wrote him a long letter.
email رسالة إلكترونية بعتلك رسالة إلكترونية. I sent you an email.

رسم VERB (IMPERFECT: يرسم)
draw بيرسم كل يوم. He draws every day.
paint رسم ورود. He painted flowers.

رسمة NOUN
drawing, painting, picture هيدي رسمة حلوة. That's a beautiful picture!

رضي VERB (IMPERFECT: يرضى)
satisfy, please الأسعار رضيت الكل.
The prices satisfied everyone.

رطب ADJECTIVE (ELATIVE: أرطب)
wet شعري رطب. My hair is wet.

رعى VERB (IMPERFECT: يرعى)
graze البقر عم يرعوا. The cows are grazing.
itch جلدا عم يرعى. His skin itches.

رف NOUN (PLURAL: رفوف)
shelf حطيت الكتاب عالرف. I put the book on the shelf.

رفض VERB (IMPERFECT: يرفض)
refuse, decline رفض يجاوب ع سؤالا.
He refused to answer her question.

رفع VERB (IMPERFECT: يرفع)
raise, lift التلميذ رفع إيدو ليجاوب.
The student raised his hand to answer.; المحل رفع أسعارو. The store raised its prices.

رفيع ADJECTIVE (ELATIVE: أرفع)
thin قصيت شقفة خبز رفيعة. I cut a thin slice of bread.

رفيق NOUN (PLURAL: رفقاة)
(male) friend رفيقي عزمني. My friend invited me.

رفقاة PLURAL NOUN (ALSO SPELLED: رفقا) (mixed group or all men) **friends** هول رفقاتي. These are my friends.

- Because a final ة is not pronounced, some people neglect to write it in this word, but its significance is seen when we add a pronoun suffix to the word, as the ة becomes ت, as in the above example.

  ⮕ See note for صاحب.

رفيقة NOUN
(female) **friend** رفيقتي عزمتني. My friend invited me.

رقبة NOUN (PLURAL: رقاب)
neck لبست عقد حول رقبتا. She wore a necklace around her neck.

رقص VERB (IMPERFECT: يرقص)
dance بحب إرقص! I love to dance!

رقصة NOUN
dance هالرقصة مشهورة. This dance is popular.

رقم NOUN (PLURAL: أرقام)
number عطاني رقمو. He gave me his number.

ركب VERB (PLURAL: يركب)
ride ركبت حصان بالمزرعة. I rode a horse on the farm.

ركبة NOUN (PLURAL: ركب)
knee البنت وقعت ع ركبتا. The girl fell on her knee.

ركض VERB (IMPERFECT: يركض)
run الأرنب بيركض بسرعة. The rabbit runs fast.

رمادي ADJECTIVE
gray إمي عندا بسينة رمادية. My mother has a gray cat.

رمز NOUN (PLURAL: رموز)
symbol, sign شو معنى هيدا الرمز؟ What does this symbol mean?

رمل NOUN (PLURAL: رمال)
sand الولاد لعبوا بالرمل. The kids played with the sand.

رمى VERB (IMPERFECT: يرمي)
throw رمى الطابة. He threw the ball.

رن VERB (IMPERFECT: يرن)
ring التلفون رن. The phone rang.

رهيب ADJECTIVE
terrible عندي أخبار منيحة وأخبار رهيبة إلك. I have good news and terrible news for you.

رياضة NOUN
exercise بتحمم بعد الرياضة. I take a shower after exercising.
sport بيحب كل أنواع الرياضة. He loves all types of sports.

ريحة NOUN (PLURAL: روايح)
smell. الريحة حلوة. The smell is nice.

ريش COLLECTIVE NOUN
feathers. ريش العصفور حلو. The bird's feathers are beautiful.

ز ز ـزـ

isolated
initial
medial
final

Zaa is the eleventh letter of the Arabic alphabet. It is pronounced z (as in the word zoo). Phonemic transcription: z

ا ب ت ث ج ح خ د ذ ر **ز** س ش ص ض ط ظ ع غ ف ق ك ل م ن ه ة و ي

زاح VERB (IMPERFECT: **يزيح**)
move (aside). زحت الكرسة. I moved the chair.

زاد VERB (IMPERFECT: **يزيد**)
rise, increase. الحرارة بتزيد بالصيفية. The temperature rises in the summer.

زار VERB (IMPERFECT: **يزور**)
visit. ما زرت جدي هالأسبوع. I haven't visited my grandfather this week.

زان VERB (IMPERFECT: **يزين**)
weigh. فيك تزين التفاح، بليز؟ Could you weigh these apples, please?

زاوية NOUN (PLURAL: **زوايا**)
(room) corner. الطاولة بزاوية الأوضة. The table is in the corner of the room.

زاير NOUN (PLURAL: **زوار**)
visitor. الزوار لح يوصلوا المسا. The visitors will arrive in the evening.

زبالة NOUN
garbage, trash, waste. حط الزبالة برا. Put the garbage outside.

زبدة NOUN (NO PLURAL)
butter. بحط دايما زبدة ع خبزتي. I always put butter on my bread.

زرع VERB (IMPERFECT: **يزرع**)
plant. ستي زرعت شجرة. My grandmother planted a tree.

زرع COLLECTIVE NOUN
plants, greenery. عندي زرع بمكتبي. I have plants in my office.

زريعة NOUN
house plant. عندي كتير زريعة ببيتي.

I have many plants in my house.

زعب VERB (IMPERFECT: **يزعب**)

fire, dismiss. زعب الموظف. He fired the employee.

زعل VERB (IMPERFECT: **يزعل**)

become sad, get upset. زعل بس حضر الأخبار. He got upset when he watched the news.

زعلان ADJECTIVE

sad, upset. هو زعلان. He is sad.

زمان ADVERB

long ago, in the olden days. زمان، كانوا النسوان يجيبوا مي من البير. In the olden days, women used to get water from the well.

من زمان a long time ago

شتريت هيدي السيارة من زمان. I bought this car a long time ago.

صارلو زمان ما (+ perfect verb) it's been a long time since…

صارلنا زمان ما شفناه. We haven't seen him in a long time.

زهر ADJECTIVE, INVARIABLE

pink. لبست فستان زهر. She wore a pink dress.

- This is an invariable adjective, which means it does not take suffixes to agree with a feminine or plural noun. In the above example, the noun is masculine, but if we replaced it with a

feminine noun, the adjective would not take the ending ـة: بلوزة زهر a pink blouse.

زهق VERB (IMPERFECT: **يزهق**)

become bored, be fed up. زهق لأنو لحالو بالبيت. He is bored because he is home alone.

زهق VERB (IMPERFECT: **يزهق**)

bore. زهق الكل لأن حكي كتير. He bored everyone because he talked so much.

زواج NOUN

marriage. بعدو بيحبا بعد كذا سنين زواج. He still loves her after many years of marriage.

زوج NOUN (PLURAL: **أزواج**)

husband. زوجا دكتور. Her husband is a doctor.

- Notice that ـه ō becomes ـو aw when a suffix is added to the word: زوج zōj → زوجا záwja

زوجة NOUN

wife. زوجتو معلمة. His wife is a teacher.

زود VERB (IMPERFECT: **يزود**)

provide, supply, equip. زودني بمعلومات جديدة. He provided me with new information.

زيادة NOUN

increase الزيادة بالزوار اليوم بسبب الطقس الحلو. The increase in visitors today is because of the nice weather.

زيارة NOUN

visit. ستمتعنا بزيارتك كتير We enjoyed your visit very much.

زيت NOUN (PLURAL: زيوت)

oil (cooking). ما بحب إطبخ بالزيت. I don't like to cook with oil.

Siin is the twelfth letter of the Arabic alphabet. It is pronounced s (as in the word six). Phonemic transcription: s

ا ب ت ث ج ح خ د ذ ر ز **س** ش ص ض ط ظ ع غ ف ق ك ل م ن ه و ي

ساحة NOUN
square, plaza في ساحة صغيرة جنب المطعم. There is a small square next to the restaurant.
yard, courtyard الولاد عم يلعبوا بالساحة. The children are playing in the yard.

يساع VERB (IMPERFECT: ساع)
fit اللعبة بتساع بالعلبة. The doll fits in the box.

ساعة NOUN
clock, watch شاف الوقت ع ساعتو. He saw the time on his watch.
hour بشوفك بعد ساعة. I'll see you in an hour.

ساعد VERB (IMPERFECT: يساعد)
help ساعدني نضف البيت. He helped me clean the house.

سافر VERB (IMPERFECT: يسافر)
travel لح يسافروا حول العالم. They're going to travel around the world.

ساق VERB (IMPERFECT: يسوق)
drive سمحوا للنسوان تسوق بالسعدية. They have allowed women to drive in Saudi Arabia.; ما بحب سوق سيارة بالليل. I don't like to drive at night.

سأل VERB (IMPERFECT: يسأل)
ask بنت لميس بتسأل كتير أسئلة. Lamees' daughter asks many questions.

سامح VERB (IMPERFECT: يسامح)
forgive عمول معروف سامحني! Please forgive me!

ساندويشة NOUN
sandwich أكلت ساندويشة جبنة عالغدا. I ate a cheese sandwich for lunch.

سبب VERB (IMPERFECT: يسبب)
cause. الشتي سبب فيضان. The rain caused a flood.

سبت NOUN (PLURAL: إيام السبت)
Saturday. ما بروح عالشغل السبت. I don't go to work on Saturday.

↪ See note for أحد.

سبح VERB (IMPERFECT: يسبح)
swim. فيك تسبح؟ Can you swim?

سبعة NUMBER
seven. بعيش بالشقة رقم سبعة. I live in apartment number seven.

↪ See note for تلاتة.

سبعتعش NUMBER
seventeen. مدرستي عالشارع رقم سبعتعش. My school is on 17th Street.

↪ See note for طنعش.

سبعين NUMBER
seventy. كرستو رقم سبعين. His seat is number seventy.

سبور NOUN (NO PLURAL)
sport. بيحب كل أنواع السبور. He loves all kinds of sports.

ست NOUN, FEMININE
grandmother. ستي حضرت كيك. My grandmother prepared a cake. الست كانت لابسة فستان أسود. lady. The lady was wearing a black dress. Mrs. هيدا مقعد ست فرح. This is Mrs. Farah's seat.

ستأجر VERB (IMPERFECT: يستأجر)
rent. ستأجرت شقة جديدة. I rented a new apartment.

ستة NUMBER
six. هيدي المدرسة بتبلش عالستة. This school starts at six.

↪ See note for تلاتة.

ستضاف VERB (IMPERFECT: يستضيف)
welcome. ستضافوا الموظفين الجداد عالشركة. They welcomed the new employees to the company.

ستعار VERB (IMPERFECT: يستعير)
borrow. ستعاروا كتير مصاري من البنك. They borrowed a lot of money from the bank.

ستعجل VERB (IMPERFECT: يستعجل)
rush, hurry. بستعجل لروح عالشغل كل يوم. I hurry to get to work every day.; ستعجل لأنو كان مأخر. He hurried because he was late.

ستعمل VERB (IMPERFECT: يستعمل)
use. بيستعمل كمبيوتر بالشغل. He uses a computer at work.

ستمتع بـ VERB (IMPERFECT: يستمتع)
enjoy. ستمتع بالحفلة. He enjoyed the party.

ستمرّ VERB (IMPERFECT: يستمرّ)
(+ imperfect verb) **continue, keep (doing)** ستمر يغني لحد ما الكل فلوا من الحفلة. He kept singing until everyone left the party.

ستّين NUMBER
sixty إمي خلقت بالستّينات. My mother was born in the '60s.

سجّل VERB (IMPERFECT: يسجّل)
record سجّل شو قالوا. He recorded what they said.
save لح سجّل رقمك. I will save your number.

سحب VERB (IMPERFECT: يسحب)
pull سحب الباب ليفتحو. He pulled the door to open it.

سحر NOUN (NO PLURAL)
charm, enchantment الكل بيحبّوا هيدا الممثّل لأن عندو سحر. Everybody loves this actor because he has charm.

سخن ADJECTIVE (ELATIVE: أسخن)
hot في آخد مشروب سخن. Can I have a hot drink?

سخّن VERB (IMPERFECT: يسخّن)
heat up, warm up بسخّن الحليب. I'm heating up the milk.

سخيف ADJECTIVE (ELATIVE: أسخف)
silly هيدي المزحة سخيفة. This joke is silly.

سدّ VERB (IMPERFECT: يسدّ)
block البناية الجديدة سدّت المنظر. The new building blocked the view.

سرّع VERB (IMPERFECT: يسرّع)
speed up, accelerate التدخين فيه يسرّع مشاكل الصحة. Smoking can accelerate health problems.

سرعة NOUN
speed معظم حوادث السيارات بتصير بسبب السرعة. Most car accidents happen because of speeding.
بسرعة ADVERB **quickly** ترك المكان بسرعة. He left the place quickly.

سرق VERB (IMPERFECT: يسرق)
steal سرقوا سيّارتو. They stole his car.
rob سرقوا البانك. They robbed the bank.

سريع ADJECTIVE (ELATIVE: أسرع)
quick, fast بدّي جواب سريع. I want a quick answer.

سطع VERB (IMPERFECT: يسطع)
touch ما تسطع وجّك! Don't touch your face!

سطعش NUMBER
sixteen في سطعش تلميذ بالصف. There are sixteen students in the class.

➲ See note for طنعش.

62 | Beginning Learner's Levantine Arabic Dictionary

سعادة NOUN (NO PLURAL)

happiness. تمنيت للعروس السعادة.
I wished the bride happiness.

سعدان (PLURAL: سعادين) NOUN

monkey. السعدان كان معلق ع شجرة.
The monkey was hanging from a tree.

السعدية NOUN (NO PLURAL)

Saudi Arabia. ما بتشتي كتير بالسعدية.
It doesn't rain a lot in Saudi Arabia.

سعر (PLURAL: أسعار) NOUN

price. الأسعار زادت هيدا الشهر.
The prices increased this month.

سفرة NOUN

trip, journey. هيدي أول سفرة إلي برا.
This is my first trip abroad.

سفينة (PLURAL: سفن) NOUN

ship. السفينة أبحرت لعدة إيام.
The ship sailed for many days.

سكت (IMPERFECT: يسكت) VERB

silence, make quiet. حمول البيبي لتسكتو. Hold the baby to silence him.

سكر NOUN (NO PLURAL)

sugar. دايما بحط سكر بقهوتي.
I always put sugar in my coffee.

سكر (IMPERFECT: يسكر) VERB

close, shut. المحل بيسكر بكير. The store closes early.

سكرت وقالت باي. hang up (phone).
She said goodbye and hung up.

سكوت NOUN (NO PLURAL)

silence. أنا بحاجة لسكوت لنام. I need silence to sleep.

سكينة (PLURAL: سكاكين) NOUN

knife. الولاد الصغار ما لازم يستعملوا سكينة. Small children shouldn't use a knife.

سلام NOUN (NO PLURAL)

peace. نحنا بحاجة لسلام بالعالم. We need peace in the world.

سلامة NOUN (NO PLURAL)

safety. سلامة الألعاب كتير مهمة. The safety of toys is very important.

سلة (PLURAL: سلال) NOUN

basket. هنادي عبت السلة تفاح. Hanadi filled the basket with apples.

سلف (IMPERFECT: يسلف) VERB

lend. بيي سلفني مصاري لإشتري سيارة.
My dad lent me money to buy a car.

سلك (PLURAL: أسلاك) NOUN

wire. ما تسطع السلك. Don't touch the wire!

سلم (PLURAL: سلالم) NOUN

ladder. ستعملت سلم لإتسلق الحيط.
I used a ladder to climb the wall.

سلى VERB (IMPERFECT: يسلي)
be fun, be entertaining. اللعبة بتسلي كتير. The game is a lot of fun.

سم NOUN (PLURAL: سموم)
poison. السم قتلو. The poison killed him.

سما NOUN, FEMININE (PLURAL: سموات)
sky. السما زرقا. The sky is blue.

سمح لـ VERB (IMPERFECT: يسمح)
allow, let. سمح لولادو يحضروا هيدا الفيلم. He let his kids watch this movie.

سمع VERB (IMPERFECT: يسمع)
hear. سمعت إسمي. I heard my name.
listen (to). الصبي ما بيسمع أهلو. The boy doesn't listen to his parents.

سمك COLLECTIVE NOUN (SINGULAR: سمكة)
fish. ما بحب السمك لأن ريحتو مش حلوة. I don't like fish because it smells bad.; البسينة أكلت السمكة. The cat ate the fish.

- Notice that we are referring to 'meat' in the first example, so the collective form is used, while in the second example, we are referring to one animal, so the singular form is used.
- ⊃ See also note for دجاج.

سميك ADJECTIVE (ELATIVE: أسمك, PLURAL: سماك)
thick. عم تقرا كتاب عنجد سميك! You're reading a really thick book!

سن NOUN (PLURAL: سنان)
tooth. سنانو صفر. His teeth are yellow.

سنة NOUN (PLURAL: سنين)
year. تجوزت هالسنة. I got married this year.

سهل ADJECTIVE (ELATIVE: أسهل)
easy. التمرين سهل. The exercise is easy.

سوا ADVERB
together. بيعيشوا سوا. They live together.

سؤال NOUN (PLURAL: أسئلة)
question. المعلمة سألت سؤال صعب. The teacher asked a difficult question.

سوبر ماركت NOUN (PLURAL: سوبر ماركات)
supermarket. لازم إشتري شي من السوبر ماركت. I need to buy something at the supermarket.

سوري INTERJECTION
sorry, excuse me, pardon. سوري، فيني إستعمل قلمك؟ Sorry, can I use your pen?

- This is borrowed from the English 'sorry.' The Lebanese have borrowed several expressions from English and French. (➲ See also, for example, باي, بليز, مرسي, and.)

سوري NOUN, ADJECTIVE

Syrian. عيلة سورية عايشة بحيي A Syrian family lives in my neighborhood.

سوريا NOUN (NO PLURAL), FEMININE

Syria. سوريا أكبر من لبنان Syria is bigger than Lebanon.

سوق NOUN (PLURAL: أسواق)

market, bazaar. السوق بيسكر الأحد The market is closed on Sunday.

- Be careful. سوق can also mean 'I drive.' (➲ See ساق)

سيارة NOUN

car. بيروح عالشغل بالسيارة He goes to work by car.

سيد NOUN (PLURAL: سيدا)

mister, Mr. سيد زياد جايي اليوم. Mr. Ziad is coming today.

سيطر ع VERB (IMPERFECT: يسيطر)

control. زوجها بيسيطر عليها Her husband controls her.

سيطرة NOUN

control, controlling. سيطرة الشرطة على المشكل كان سريع The police took control of the fight quickly.

- This is the verbal noun of the verb سيطر. A verbal noun expresses the idea of the action of the verb as a subject or object and is analogous to the gerund (-ing form) in English. The above example could more literally be translated as 'The police's controlling of the fight was quick.'

سيف NOUN (PLURAL: سيوف)

sword. وقع سيفو He dropped his sword.

سيكس NOUN (NO PLURAL)

sex. بياخدوا تعليم سيكس بالمدرسة. They take sex education at school.

سيلولير NOUN

cell phone. نسيت سيلوليري بالبيت. I forgot my cell phone at home.

سينما NOUN, FEMININE (PLURAL: سينمايات)

cinema, movies. السينما القديمة كانت بالأبيض والأسود Old movies were in black and white.

movie theater, cinema. بروح عالسينما كل أحد I go to the movies every Sunday.

ش شـ ـشـ ـش

isolated / initial / medial / final

Shiin is the thirteenth letter of the Arabic alphabet. It is pronounced *sh* (as in the word **sh**ow). Phonemic transcription: š

ا ب ت ث ج ح خ د ذ ر ز س **ش** ص ض ط ظ ع غ ف ق ك ل م ن ه و ي

شابو NOUN

cap. لبس شابو ليحمي حالو من الشمس. He wore a cap to protect himself from the sun.

- This word is borrowed from the French 'chapeau.' Levantine Arabic has borrowed many words from French and English, especially those related to technology, fashion, and foreign food.

شارع NOUN (PLURAL: شوارع)

street. ع أي شارع عايش؟ What street do you live on?

شارك VERB (IMPERFECT: يشارك)

participate, take part. المعلمة بدا كل تلاميذا يشاركوا. The teacher wants all of her students to participate.

شاف VERB (IMPERFECT: يشوف)

see. ما شفتو بالحفلة. I didn't see him at the party.

شال VERB (IMPERFECT: يشيل)

remove, take off. شال صباطو. He removed his shoes.

شامل ADJECTIVE (ELATIVE: أشمل)

general. عطيني جواب شامل ع سؤالي. Give me a general answer to my question.

شاي NOUN

tea. هيدا الشاي طيب! This tea is delicious!

شباط NOUN (NO PLURAL)

February. لح يسافر بشباط. He will travel in February.

شباك NOUN (PLURAL: **شبابيك**)

بليز، سكر الشباك. Please, close the window. **window**

شبك NOUN

السمكة كانت بقلب الشبك. The fish was inside the net. **net**

شتاق لـ VERB (IMPERFECT: **يشتاق**)

شتقت لبي. I miss my dad. **miss**

شتت VERB (IMPERFECT: **تشتي**)

شتت اليوم. It rained today. **rain**

- Theoretically, the base form of this verb would be شتى, but it is always feminine because the unexpressed but implied subject is الدنيا (the weather).

شترى VERB (IMPERFECT: **يشتري**)

ما بدي إشتري أي شي هون. **buy** I don't want to buy anything here.

شتغل VERB (IMPERFECT: **يشتغل**)

بيشتغلوا كلن ببيروت. They all **work** work in Beirut.; بيشتغل ست ساعات كل يوم. He works six hours every day.

شتوي ADJECTIVE

ببقا بالبيت بالإيام الشتوية. I stay **rainy** at home on rainy days.

- Notice that the feminine form of the adjective in the above example is identical to the noun in the following entry. Context will make the meaning clear.

شتوية NOUN

ما بحب الشتوية. كتير بارد. **winter** I don't like winter. It's too cold.

- The word for 'winter' is taken from the adjective for 'rainy,' as it is the rainy season.

شتي NOUN (NO PLURAL) (ALSO: **شتا**)

ما رحنا عالبحر بسبب الشتي. We **rain** didn't go to the beach because of the rain.

شجاع ADJECTIVE (ELATIVE: **أشجع**)

لازم تكون شجاع بهيك أوقات. **brave** You have to be brave at times like this.

شجر COLLECTIVE NOUN (SINGULAR: **شجرة**)

خلينا نقعد بالفي تحت الشجرة. **trees** Let's sit in the shade of the tree.

شخص NOUN (PLURAL: **أشخاص**)

مروان شخص منيح. Marwan is **person** a nice person.

شخطورة NOUN (PLURAL: **شخاطير**)

السمكة نطت عالشخطورة. The **boat** fish jumped into the boat.

شد VERB (IMPERFECT: **يشد**)

الصبي شد دنب البسينة. The boy **pull** pulled the cat's tail.

شراع NOUN

شراع الشخطورة أبيض. The sail of **sail** the boat is white.

شرب VERB (IMPERFECT: يشرب)
drink. بيشرب كتير عصاير He drinks a lot of juice.

شرح VERB (IMPERFECT: يشرح)
explain. الحكيم شرح الوضع. The doctor explained the case.

شرط NOUN (PLURAL: شروط)
condition, stipulation. الشركة حطت شروط لقبول موظفين جداد. The company put conditions on accepting new employees.

شرطة NOUN (NO PLURAL)
police. الشرطة وقفت الشخص المش منيح. The police stopped the bad person.

- شرطة is grammatically singular but refers to police (in a collective sense), while شرطي is one police officer. (⮕ See شرطي).

شرطي NOUN (NO PLURAL)
police officer, cop. الشرطي وقفني لأن كنت عم سوق بسرعة. The police officer pulled me over because I was speeding.

- Instead of using a plural form of this word, شرطة is usually used. (⮕ See شرطة).

شرق VERB (IMPERFECT: يشرق)
(sun) rise. الشمس بتشرق من الشرق. The sun rises in the east.

- This verb is almost exclusively used with the subject الشمس, which is feminine.

شرق NOUN (NO PLURAL)
east. سوريا ع شرق لبنان. Syria is to the east of Lebanon.

شركة NOUN
company. منشتغل بشركة صغيرة ببيروت. We work at a small company in Beirut.

شريف ADJECTIVE (ELATIVE: أشرف)
noble, honorable, respected. هيدا الرجال من عيلة شريفة. This man is from a respected family.

شريك NOUN (PLURAL: شركا)
partner. شريكي بيساعدني. My partner helps me.

- This word, like its English translation, can mean a business associate or a romantic partner. As with other words denoting people, the basic noun refers to a man, while ة is added to refer to a woman: شريكة (female partner)

شط NOUN (PLURAL: شواطئ)
beach. الولاد بيلعبوا بالرمل عالشط. Children play with sand on the beach.

شعب NOUN (PLURAL: شعوب)
public, people. الشعب بدو يعرف كل

شي. The public wants to know everything.

الشعب اللبناني Lebanese people أكترية الشعب اللبناني بيحكي تلات لغات. Most Lebanese speak three languages.

شعر NOUN

hair. عندا شعر طويل She has long hair.

شغل NOUN (PLURAL: **أشغال**)

work. عندي كتير شغل أعملو اليوم I have a lot of work to do today. job. لقت شغل بشركة منيحة She found a job at a good company. business. بلشوا شغل عائلي They started a family business.

شغلة NOUN

thing. أحسن شغلة تساعدا The best thing is to help her.

شفة NOUN (PLURAL: **شفاف**)

lip. شفافا زرق لأنا بردانة Her lips are blue because she is cold.

شقة NOUN (PLURAL: **شقق**)

apartment. الشقة بتحتوي تلات غرف The apartment consists of three rooms.

شقفة NOUN (PLURAL: **شقف**)

piece, slice. أكلت شقفة بيتزا I ate a slice of pizza.

شكرا INTERJECTION

thanks, thank you. شكرا! إنت لطيف Thanks! That's kind of you!

شكل NOUN (PLURAL: **أشكال**)

shape, form. البنت الصغيرة فيا ترسم أشكال The little girl can draw shapes.

شكل VERB (IMPERFECT: **يشكل**)

shape, form. شكلت المعجون She shaped the clay.

شم VERB (IMPERFECT: **يشم**)

smell. شميت الورود I smelled the flower.

شمال

NOUN (NO PLURAL) north. رفيقتي من شمال لبنان My friend is from the north of Lebanon.
NOUN (NO PLURAL) left. بيتي عالشمال My house is on the left.; السيارة لفت عالشمال The car turned left.
ADJECTIVE, INVARIABLE. ضربت الميلة الشمال من سيارتي I hit the left side of my car.

شمس NOUN (NO PLURAL), FEMININE

sun. ما تتطلع عالشمس! Don't look at the sun!

شمعة NOUN (PLURAL: **شموع**)

candle. حطيت شموع عالطاولة I put candles on the table.

شَنْطَة NOUN (PLURAL: شنط)

bag. باخد شنطة وحدة بس لمن سافر.
I take only one bag when I travel.

شَهْر NOUN (PLURAL: أشهر)

month. عيد ميلادي هيدا الشهر. My birthday is this month.

شو PRONOUN

what. شو هيدا؟ What is this?

شو ما كان anything, whatever. بدي إحضر شو ما كان عالتلفزيون. I want to watch whatever on TV.

شُوبِينْغ NOUN (NO PLURAL)

shopping. راحت شوبينغ. She went shopping.

شُورَبَة NOUN

soup. الشوربة سخنة. The soup is hot.

شَوْكَة NOUN

fork. الصبي فيه ياكل بالشوكة. The child can eat with a fork.

شُوكُولا NOUN (ALSO: شوكولاتا)

chocolate. أكل الشوكولا بيزيد السعادة. Eating chocolate increases happiness.

شْوَي ADVERB

a (little) bit. ذاكرة ستي ضعيفة شوي. My grandmother's memory is a bit weak.

شوي شوي slowly. بليز سوق شوي شوي. Please drive slowly.

شْوَيّة DETERMINER

a little bit (of). بيحكي شوية ألماني. He speaks a little German.

شِي

NOUN (PLURAL: أشيا) thing, object. شو هالشي؟ What is this thing?; أحسن شي تساعدا. The best thing is to help her.

DETERMINER (+ noun) some. إذا رحت شي مرة ع إيطاليا، لح إبعتلك صور. If I go to Italy sometime, I will send you a photo.

DETERMINER (+ number) around, about, approximately. سافرت إيطاليا من شي خمس سنين. I traveled to Italy some five years ago.

PARTICLE (yes/no question +) عندا هي ولاد شي؟ Does she have children?

- A yes/no question in Levantine Arabic can be formed by adding شي to the end of the sentence, as in the last example above. It is also common to omit the شي, in which case the question is identical to a statement, with only the intonation or punctuation letting us know that it is, in fact, a question. Compare the following statement and question: هي عندا ولاد. She has children.; هي عندا ولاد؟ Does she have children?

70 | Beginning Learner's Levantine Arabic Dictionary

PRONOUN **something** بدي آكل شي.
I want to eat something.

anything, whatever أي شي
بدي إحضر أي شي عالتلفزيون. I want to watch whatever on TV.

nothing ما شي   ما شي صعب إلو.
Nothing is difficult for him.

Ṣaad is the fourteenth letter of the Arabic alphabet. It is the dark counterpart of the letter س s. By 'dark,' we mean that the tongue is flattened and pulled back slightly. This affects the quality of adjacent vowels, most notably alif and fatha (➲ See notes on p. 2) Phonemic transcription: ṣ

ا ب ت ث ج ح خ د ذ ر ز س ش **ص** ض ط ظ ع غ ف ق ك ل م ن ه و ي

صابون NOUN (PLURAL: صوابين)

soap. بغسل إيدي بالصابون I wash my hands with soap.

صاحب NOUN (PLURAL: صحاب)

(male) friend. صاحبي عزمني My friend invited me.

صحاب PLURAL NOUN (mixed group or all men) friends. هول صحابي These are my friends.

- While the singular form of this masculine noun refers to one friend who is male, as with other nouns denoting humans, the plural can refer to a group of people who are all men or a mixed group of men and women. In contrast, for the feminine form of this noun below, the plural only denotes a group of all women.

صاحبة NOUN

(female) friend. صاحبتي عزمتني My friend invited me.

- Sometimes the voweling of a word changes when a suffix is added. Compare the placement of kasra (ِ) and sukuun (ْ): صاحبة ṣáḥbi → صاحبتي ṣaḥíbti

صاحي ADJECTIVE

(weather) fair. الطقس صاحي The weather is fair.

صاخن ADJECTIVE

ill, sick, unwell. ما رحت عالشغل لأني صاخنة. I didn't go to work because I'm sick.

صار VERB (IMPERFECT: يصير)

become. الصبي بدو يصير حكيم The boy wants to become a doctor. happen. الأخطاء بتصير Mistakes

72 | Beginning Learner's Levantine Arabic Dictionary

happen.

صارلو... (+ present participle) **have been __ing for...** صارلي كم سنة عايشة بلبنان. I've been living in Lebanon for a few years.; صارلنا نص ساعة ناطرين. We've been waiting for half an hour.

ما صارلو... (+ perfect tense verb) **haven't __ in..., it's been... since** صارلي سنة ما شفتا. I haven't seen her in a year. / It's been a year since I saw her.

صافي ADJECTIVE (ELATIVE: **أصفى**) **clear, pure** المي كتير صافية. The water is very clear.

صالة NOUN **hall** الصف بآخر الصالة. The classroom is at the end of the hall.

صبّ VERB (IMPERFECT: **يصبّ**) **pour** فيك بليز تصبّلي قهوة؟ Can you please pour me some coffee?

صبّاط NOUN (PLURAL: **صبابيط**) **(pair of) shoes** نضفت صبابيطي. I cleaned my shoes.

صبح NOUN (NO PLURAL) **morning** **الصبح** **in the morning, a.m.** بفيق بكير الصبح. I wake up early in the morning.

صبي NOUN (PLURAL: **صبيان**) **The**

boy الصبيان عم يلعبوا بالشارع. The boys are playing in the street.

صحافة NOUN (NO PLURAL) **press, media, journalism** الصحافة غطّت القصة. The press covered the story.

صحة NOUN (NO PLURAL) **health** الصحة أهم من المصاري. Health is more important than money.

صحّح VERB (IMPERFECT: **يصحّح**) **correct** عمول معروف، صحّحلي أخطائي. Please, correct my mistakes.

صحن NOUN (PLURAL: **صحون**) **plate, dish** حطّ الأكل ع صحن حلو. He placed the food on a beautiful plate.

dish (food) بستعمل خلطة خضرة لهيدا الصحن. I use a mix of vegetables for this dish.

صحّي ADJECTIVE **healthy** بياكل صحّي. He eats healthy.

صحيح ADJECTIVE (ALSO: **صح**) (ELATIVE: **أصح**) **correct, right** جوابك صح! Your answer is right!

صخر NOUN (PLURAL: **صخور**) **rock, stone** تخبّى ورا صخرة. He hid behind a rock.

73 | Beginning Learner's Levantine Arabic Dictionary

صدّق VERB (IMPERFECT: يصدّق)

صدّق شو قالت He believed what she said. **believe**.

- The ص in this particular word is pronounced س in Levantine Arabic, but most people retain the spelling from Modern Standard Arabic.

صرف VERB (IMPERFECT: يصرف)

صرف كل مصرياتو He spent all his money. **spend**.

صرف العملة NOUN (NO PLURAL)

المصرف خفض أسعار صرف العملة. The bank has decreased the currency exchange rates. **currency exchange**

صطدم VERB (IMPERFECT: يصطدم)

الشختورة صطدمت بالجزيرة. The boat crashed into the island. **crash**.

صعب ADJECTIVE (ELATIVE: أصعب)

التمرين صعب. The exercise is difficult. **difficult, hard**.

صغير ADJECTIVE (ELATIVE: أصغر, PLURAL: صغار)

بحب الولاد الصغار. I love small children.; عندي بسينة صغيرة. I have a little cat. **small, little**.
الصبي الصغير مهذب. The young boy is polite. **young**.

- The ص in this particular word is often pronounced ز in Levantine Arabic. Some people retain the common spelling with ص from Modern Standard Arabic, while some may write زغير to reflect the actual pronunciation.

صفّ¹ VERB (IMPERFECT: يصفّ)

صفّ جنب سيارتي. He parked next to my car. **park**.

صفّ² NOUN (PLURAL: صفوف)

الصف فيه عشر تلاميذ. There are ten students in the class. **class, classroom**.

صفحة NOUN

علمت الصفحة تمانة من الكتاب. She marked page 8 of the book. **page**.

صفر NUMBER (PLURAL: صفار)

لازم نبلش من الصفر. We have to start from zero. **zero**.

صفر VERB (IMPERFECT: يصفر)

بيصفر بس يمرض. He turns yellow when he gets sick. **turn yellow**.

صلح VERB (IMPERFECT: يصلح)

صلح الكرسة المكسورة. He repaired the broken chair. **repair, fix**.
عمول معروف، صلحلي أخطائي. Please, correct my mistakes. **correct**.

صوت NOUN (PLURAL: أصوات)

سمعت صوت غريب. I heard a strange noise. **sound, noise**.
فيك تعلي الصوت؟ Can you turn up the volume? **volume**.

voice عندا صوت حلو. She has a lovely voice.

صوّر VERB (IMPERFECT: يصوّر) photograph, take a picture (of) بحب صور الحيوانات. I like to photograph animals.

صورة NOUN (PLURAL: صور) photo بياخد صور حلوة. He takes beautiful photos.

picture البنت لوّنت الصورة. The girl colored the picture.

صيف NOUN (PLURAL: صيفيات) summer شو عملت الصيف الماضي؟ What did you do last summer?

صيفية NOUN summer شو عملت الصيفية الماضية؟ What did you do last summer?

Ḍaad is the fifteenth letter of the Arabic alphabet. It is the dark counterpart of the letter د d. To better understand the contrast between light and dark consonants, compare the place of articulation for the light L in the English word leak and the dark L in word dull. (➲ See notes for ص.) Phonemic transcription: **ḍ**

ا ب ت ث ج ح خ د ذ ر ز س ش ص **ض** ط ظ ع غ ف ق ك ل م ن ه و ي

ضبط VERB (IMPERFECT: **يضبط**)
control. ضبط إحساسو. He controlled his emotions.

ضجة NOUN
noise. الضجة فيقت البيبي. The noise woke the baby.

ضحك VERB (IMPERFECT: **يضحك**)
laugh. ضحك ولو إنو المزحة مش مهضومة. He laughed even though the joke wasn't funny.
ضحك ع laugh at, make fun of, fool. ما تخلي حدا يضحك عليك. Don't let anybody fool you.

ضحك VERB (IMPERFECT: **يضحك**)
make laugh. القصة ضحكتني. The story made me laugh.

ضخم ADJECTIVE (ELATIVE: **أضخم**, PLURAL: **ضخام**)
enormous, huge. شترى كمية بضاعة ضخمة. He bought an enormous amount of merchandise.

ضرب VERB (IMPERFECT: **يضرب**)
hit. الولد الصغير ضرب رفيقو. The young boy hit his friend.

ضربة NOUN
blow, strike. الضربة ع راسو كانت قوية. The blow to his head was strong.

ضروري
ADJECTIVE necessary, required. عندي كل الأدوات الضرورية لإبني علبة. I have all the necessary tools to build a box.
PSEUDO-VERB, INVARIABLE (+ imperfect verb) need, have to. أنت مريض، ضروري تروح عالمستشفى. You're sick. You have to go to the hospital!
مش ضروري don't have to

ضروري You don't ضروري تعملو إذا ما بدك. have to do that if you don't want to.

- This word is synonymous with لازم in positive sentences. However, compare its meaning with those of لازم in negative sentences. (See ⇨ لازم)

ضعيف ADJECTIVE (ELATIVE: أضعف, PLURAL: ضعاف)
weak. جدي ضعيف My grandpa is weak.
low. الفرصة إنا تشتي ضعيف The chance that it will rain is low.

ضل VERB (IMPERFECT: يضل)
stay. ضليت بالبيت كل النهار I stayed home all day.

ضهر NOUN (PLURAL: ضهور)
back. ضهري بيوجعني بعد الرياضة My back hurts me after exercising.

ضهر VERB (IMPERFECT: يضهر)
go out. ما بدي إضهر، بدي إبقى بالبيت. I don't want to go out. I want to stay home.

ضو NOUN (PLURAL: أضوية)
light. طفي الضو، بليز Turn off the light, please.

- Both ـَو aw and final ـَوّ aww are pronounced as the diphthong aw. Remember that a final doubled consonant is really only pronounced double when followed by a suffix beginning in a vowel.

ضوي VERB (IMPERFECT: يضوي)
light up, illuminate. استعملت شموع لضوي الأوضة. I used candles to light up the room.
turn on. ضوى الكمبيوتر. He turned on the computer.

ضيع VERB (IMPERFECT: يضيع)
lose, misplace. ضيعت خاتما. She lost her ring.
waste. ضيعت وقتي! I wasted my time!

- The perfect tense conjugation for both 'she' and 'I' is written ـت, but the verb's stress pattern is different. Listen carefully to the audio: ḍáyya3it vs. ḍayyá3it.

ضيعة NOUN (PLURAL: ضيع)
village. الحياة رايقة بالضيعة. Life is tranquil in the village.

ضيف NOUN (PLURAL: ضيوف)
guest. كان في كتير ضيوف بالعرس. There were many guests at the wedding.

ضيف VERB (IMPERFECT: يضيف)
serve. ضيف فواكه بعد الغدا. He served fruit after dinner.

ضيق ADJECTIVE (ELATIVE: أضيق)
narrow. الممر ضيق. The hall is narrow.
tight. هيدا بنطلون كتير ضيق. These pants are too tight.

ط ط ط ط
final medial initial isolated

Ṭaa is the sixteenth letter of the Arabic alphabet. It is the dark counterpart of the letter ت t. (➲ See notes for ص and ض for more on dark letters.) Phonemic transcription: *ṭ*

ا ب ت ث ج ح خ د ذ ر ز س ش ص ض **ط** ظ ع غ ف ق ك ل م ن ه و ي

طابة NOUN
ball. إبن توفيق بدو يلعب بالطابة.
Tawfik's son wants to play with the ball.

طابع NOUN (PLURAL: طوابع)
stamp. عندي مجموعة طوابع من كل بلد.
I have a collection of stamps from every country.

طار VERB (IMPERFECT: يطير)
fly. العصفور بيطير بالسما. The bird flies in the sky.

طارد VERB (IMPERFECT: يطارد)
chase. الكلب طارد البسينة. The dog chased the cat.

طازة ADJECTIVE, INVARIABLE
fresh. بشتري بس فواكه طازة. I only buy fresh fruit.

طاع VERB (IMPERFECT: يطيع)
obey. التلاميذ لازم يطيعوا القوانين.
Students should obey the rules.

طاولة NOUN
table. خلينا نقعد عالطاولة تاكل. Let's sit at the table to eat.

طب NOUN (NO PLURAL)
medicine. إبني بدو يدرس طب. My son wants to study medicine.

طباخ NOUN
cook, chef. المطعم عندو طباخ إيطالي.
The restaurant has an Italian chef.

- When a plural form is not listed for a noun, you can assume that its plural is regular. For masculine human nouns, as this one, the regular plural ending is ـين: طباخين (chefs)
- Most masculine human nouns can

78 | Beginning Learner's Levantine Arabic Dictionary

be made feminine by adding the ending ـة. طباخ (male chef) → طباخة (female chef). The masculine plural (طباخين) can refer to a group of all male chefs or a mixed group, while 'female chefs' is طباخات.

طبخ VERB (IMPERFECT: يطبخ)
cook. ما بدي إطبخ شي اليوم. I don't want to cook anything today.

طبق NOUN (PLURAL: طباق)
plate, dish. حط الأكل ع طبق حلو. He placed the food on a beautiful plate.

طبقة NOUN
(school) desk. نسي كتابو بطبقة المدرسة. He forgot his book in his school desk.

طبيعة NOUN
nature. بحب أفلام عن الطبيعة. I like documentaries about nature.
nature, character, disposition. هيدا الكلب عندو طبيعة حلوة. This dog has a good nature.

طحين NOUN (NO PLURAL)
flour. بدي طحين لأعمل كيك. I need flour to make a cake.

طرح VERB (IMPERFECT: يطرح)
introduce. طرح الإستاذ موضوع مهم للنقاش. The teacher introduced an important topic for discussion.

طرد VERB (IMPERFECT: يطرد)
fire, dismiss. طرد الموظف. He fired the employee.

طرف NOUN (PLURAL: طراف)
side. الدائرة ما عندا طراف. A circle doesn't have sides.
edge, margin, border. رسمت ع طرف الورقة. She drew in the margin of the paper.

طري ADJECTIVE
soft. شتريت للبيبي لعبة طرية. I bought the baby a soft toy.

طريق NOUN (PLURAL: طرقات)
road, path. في شجر جنب الطريق. There are trees along the road.
way, route. بيتي من هالطريق! My house is this way!

طريقة NOUN (PLURAL: طرق)
method, way. المعلمة فرجت الصبي الطريقة ليكتب إسمو. The teacher showed the boy the way to write his name.

طعمى VERB (IMPERFECT: يطعمي)
feed. طعمت البيبي. She fed the baby.

طفل NOUN (PLURAL: أطفال)
child, baby. الطفل عم يلعب بالجنينة. The child is playing in the garden.

79 | Beginning Learner's Levantine Arabic Dictionary

طفى VERB (IMPERFECT: يطفي)

turn off طفيت الضو؟ Did you turn off the light?

طقس NOUN (PLURAL: طقوس)

weather. الطقس مش منيح The weather is bad.

طقية NOUN

cap (hat) لبس طقية ليحمي حالو من الشمس. He wore a cap to protect himself from the sun.

طلب VERB (IMPERFECT: يطلب)

order. طلبت أكل She ordered food.

طلبية NOUN

order. الطلبية وصلت اليوم The order arrived today.

طلع VERB (IMPERFECT: يطلع)

get on, get in, board طلع عالطيارة. He got on the plane.

طنعش NUMBER

twelve شتريت طنعش بيضة من المحل. I bought twelve eggs at the store.

- When the numbers 11-19 precede a noun, 1) the noun is singular; 2) ر -ar- is added to the number.

طول NOUN (NO PLURAL)

length شو طول الفيلم؟ What is the length of the movie?
height. طول هيدا الجبل كبير The height of this mountain is great.

طوى VERB (IMPERFECT: يطوي)

fold طوى الورقة. He folded the paper.

طويل ADJECTIVE (ELATIVE: أطول, PLURAL: طوال)

long شعرا طويل She has long hair.
tall عمو رجال طويل. His uncle is a tall man.

طيارة NOUN

plane سافرت بالطيارة. I traveled by plane.

طيب[1] ADJECTIVE (ELATIVE: أطيب)

delicious الأكل كتير طيب. The food is very delicious.

طيب[2] INTERJECTION

okay, all right طيب، لح إجي بكرا! Okay, I will come tomorrow!

80 | Beginning Learner's Levantine Arabic Dictionary

Ẓaa is the seventeenth letter of the Arabic alphabet. It is the dark counterpart of the letter ز z. (➲ See notes for ص and ض for more on dark letters.) This letter is rather uncommon in Levantine Arabic and is replaced in some words by ز or ض. Phonemic transcription: ẓ

ا ب ت ث ج ح خ د ذ ر ز س ش ص ض ط **ظ** ع غ ف ق ك ل م ن ه و ي

ظل NOUN (PLURAL: **ظلول**)

بحب إقعد بالظل. I like to sit in the shade. **shade**.

ظلّل VERB (IMPERFECT: **يظلّل**)

ظللت شبابيكي. I shaded my windows. **shade**.

81 | Beginning Learner's Levantine Arabic Dictionary

ع ـع ـعـ عـ
isolated
initial
medial
final

'Ayn is the eighteenth letter of the Arabic alphabet. It is the voiced equivalent of the letter ح ḥ and has no equivalent in English. Rather than try to follow a complicated explanation of how to produce this sound, it is better to listen carefully to the audio tracks and mimic what you hear. Phonemic transcription: **3**

ا ب ت ث ج ح خ د ذ ر ز س ش ص ض ط ظ **ع** غ ف ق ك ل م ن ه و ي

ع PREPOSITION (ALSO SPELLED: عـ, ALSO: على)

on الأكل عالطاولة. The food is on the table.
to الولاد بيروحوا عالمدرسة الصبح. The children go to school in the morning.

I	علي 3aláyyi	WE	علينا 3aláyna	
YOU M.	عليك 	YOU PL.	عليكن 	
YOU F.	عليكي 			
HE	عليه 3alē(h)	THEY	علين 3aláyun	
SHE	عليا 3aláya			

ع مهلو ADVERB (+ pronoun suffix) **slowly**
بليز سوق ع مهلك. Please drive slowly.

- Keep in mind that Levantine Arabic does not have official, standardized spelling. Some people write ع as a separate word, while others prefix it to the following word. In this book, we only prefix it to the definite article: عال.

عائلي ADJECTIVE

family- هيدي مشكلة عائلية. It's a family problem.

- This is a nisba adjective (➲ See note for حقيقي). It creates an adjective from a noun and means 'related to __' or 'having to do with __.'

عاد[1] VERB (IMPERFECT: يعيد)

repeat عادت نفس الغلطة. She repeated the same mistake.

- Notice that there are two separate verbs with the identical base forms عاد but different conjugations.

عاد[2] VERB (IMPERFECT: يعود)

return, go back, come back عاد من الشغل بعد الضهر. He returned from work in the afternoon.

عادة NOUN

habit, custom التدخين عادة مش منيحة. Smoking is a bad habit.

بالعادة ADVERB (ALSO: عادة) usually باخد بالعادة تاكسي عالشغل. I usually take a taxi to work.

عادل ADJECTIVE (ELATIVE: أعدل)

fair المباراة كانت عادلة. The game was fair.

عار VERB (IMPERFECT: يعير)

lend فيك تعيرني سيارتك؟ Can you lend me your car?

عارضة أزياء NOUN

fashion model بتشتغل كعارضة أزياء. She works as a model.

عاش VERB (IMPERFECT: يعيش)

live بيعيشوا مع بعض. They live together.

عاصفة NOUN (PLURAL: عواصف)

storm العاصفة دمرت البيت. The storm damaged the house.

عاقل ADJECTIVE (ELATIVE: أعقل)

wise إنت رجال عاقل! You're a wise man!

عالم NOUN (PLURAL: عوالم)

world اللبنانية بيعيشوا حول العالم. Lebanese live all over the world.

عالي ADJECTIVE (ELATIVE: أعلى)

high الحيط عالي. The wall is high.

عام ADJECTIVE

public هيدا البحر العام مجاني. This public beach is free.

عام VERB (IMPERFECT: يعوم)

float الصبي تعلم كيف يعوم. The boy learned how to float.

عبر PREPOSITION

across, over الخبر منتشر عبر القارات. The news has spread across the continents.

عبى VERB (IMPERFECT: يعبي)

fill عبى القنينة مي. I filled the bottle with water.

- This verb has two objects, whereas English would require the preposition 'with' before the second object.

عتمة NOUN (NO PLURAL)

dark ما فيي شوف بالعتمة. I can't see in the dark.

عتمد ع VERB (IMPERFECT: **يعتمد**)
depend on. السعر بيعتمد عالكمية
The price depends on the quantity.

عجيبة NOUN (PLURAL: **عجايب**)
wonder, marvel في سبع عجايب بالعالم. There are seven wonders in the world.

عد VERB (IMPERFECT: **يعد**)
count. الصبي بيقدر يعد للعشرة. The boy can count to ten.

عدد NOUN (PLURAL: **أعداد**)
number, figure عدد الناس بالعالم عم يزيد. The number of people in the world is increasing.

عدو NOUN (PLURAL: **أعداء**)
enemy. حارب العدو. He fought the enemy.

عربي NOUN (NO PLURAL)
Arabic. ما بحكي عربي منيح. I don't speak Arabic well.
Levantine Arabic عربي شامي بعلم عربي شامي. I teach Levantine Arabic.

عرس NOUN (PLURAL: **أعراس**)
wedding. عرسن بالصيف. Their wedding is in the summer.

عرض VERB (IMPERFECT: **يعرض**)
introduce عرض الإستاذ موضوع مهم للنقاش. The teacher introduced an important topic for discussion.

عرض (PLURAL: **عروض**)
display, show عرض الأسعار مش مزبوط. The display of prices is not correct.
offer, proposal ليش رفضت عرضن؟ Why did you refuse their offer?
width, breadth قست عرض التخت. I measured the width of the bed.

عرف VERB (IMPERFECT: **يعرف**)
know. ستي بتعرف كيف تطبخ أكل صحي. My grandma knows how to cook healthy food.

عرف VERB (IMPERFECT: **يعرف**)
introduce عرفني ع أهلو. He introduced me to his parents.

عروسة NOUN (PLURAL: **عرايس**)
bride. العروسة شكلا حلو بهالفستان. The bride looks beautiful in that dress!
pita wrap __ **عروسة** _ (sandwich) أكلت عروسة جبنة عالغدا. I had a pita wrap with cheese for lunch.

- The type of pita wrap is almost always specified. Some popular varieties are 'cheese,' as in the example, **عروسة لبنة** (yoghurt), and **عروسة زعتر** (thyme). Why does this sandwich take its name from 'bride'? Perhaps because the layers of rolled up flatbread resemble the layers of a bride's wedding dress!

عزم VERB (IMPERFECT: يعزم)
invite. عزمت رفقاتي عالعشا I invited my friends to dinner.

عشا NOUN (PLURAL: عشاوات)
dinner. باكل العشا مأخر. I eat dinner late.

عشان CONJUNCTION
because. الصبي تعبان عشانو مريض. The boy is tired because he is ill.

عشان هيك ADVERB therefore, so
شتت، عشان هيك بقيت بالبيت. It rained, so I stayed at home.

- A pronoun suffix can be added to the conjunction, as in the example sentence. ➲ See note for لان.

عشب NOUN (PLURAL: أعشاب)
grass. العشب أخضر. The grass is green.

عشرة NUMBER
ten. خمسة وخمسة بيعملوا عشرة. Five plus five makes ten.

عشرين NUMBER
twenty. تزوجوا من عشرين سنة. They got married twenty years ago.

عصر NOUN (PLURAL: عصور)
era, century. المدينة تغيرت عبر العصور. The city changed over the centuries.

عصري ADJECTIVE
modern. شترت فرش عصري. She bought modern furniture.

عصفور NOUN (PLURAL: عصافير)
bird. العصفور عم يغني عالشجرة. The bird is singing in the tree.

عصير NOUN (PLURAL: عصاير)
juice. ما بشرب كتير مي، بفضل العصير. I don't drink a lot of water; I prefer juice.

عضمة NOUN (PLURAL: عضام)
bone. الكلب لقى عضمة بالرمل عالبحر. The dog found a bone in the sand at the beach.

عضو NOUN (PLURAL: أعضاء)
member. أعضاء الفريق بيشتغلوا مع بعض. The members of the team work together.

عطلة NOUN (PLURAL: عطل)
vacation. أنا عنجد بحاجة لعطلة! I really need a vacation! شو عامل بالعطلة؟ weekend What are you doing on the weekend?

عطى VERB (IMPERFECT: يعطي)
give. عطيني المفاتيح. Give me the keys.

عفش NOUN (NO PLURAL)
furniture. ستي شترت عفش جديد. My grandma bought new furniture.

عفواً INTERJECTION

excuse me, sorry عفواً، فيني إستعمل قلمك؟ Sorry, can I use your pen?

عقد (PLURAL: عقود)

necklace لابسة عقد غالي. She is wearing an expensive necklace.

عقل NOUN (PLURAL: عقول)

mind الرياضة منيحة للجسم والعقل. Exercise is good for the body and the mind.

عكس NOUN (NO PLURAL)

opposite بنتي عملت عكس شو قلتلا. My daughter did the opposite of what I told her.

علامة NOUN

mark, sign, symbol خيي عندو علامة ع خدو اليمين. My brother has a mark on his right cheek.
grade, score التلميذ أخد علامة مش منيحة عالإمتحان. The student got a bad score on the examination.

علبة NOUN (PLURAL: علب)

box خبت المصاري بعلبة صغيرة. She hid the money in a little box.

علق VERB (IMPERFECT: يعلق)

hang علق الصورة فوق الطولة. Hang the picture above the table.

علم NOUN (PLURAL: أعلام)

flag علم لبنان أحمر، أبيض و أخضر. The flag of Lebanon is red, white, and green.

علم NOUN (PLURAL: علوم)

science, knowledge بحب إدرس علم الكمبيوتر. I like to study computer science.
education العلم كتير منيح بأوروبا. Education is very good in Europe.

علم VERB (IMPERFECT: يعلم)

teach بعلم إنجليزي. I teach English.
mark, label علمت إسم إبني عالقنينة. I marked my child's name on the bottle.

علني ADJECTIVE

public بدو يعطي خطاب علني. He wants to give a public speech.

على PREPOSITION (ALSO: ع)

on الأكل على الطاولة. The food is on the table.
to الولاد بيروحوا على المدرسة الصبح. The children go to school in the morning.

على VERB (IMPERFECT: يعلي)

raise, elevate, lift up المحل على أسعارو. The store raised its prices.

عم PARTICLE

(+ imperfect or bi-imperfect verb) **be ___ing** شو عم تعمل هلأ؟ What are you doing now?; ما عم باكل منيح بهالأيام. I'm not eating well

86 | Beginning Learner's Levantine Arabic Dictionary

these days.

- This particle is more commonly followed by a (bare) imperfect verb (with the prefix بـ) in many regions of the Levant, including Beirut, the dialect of which this dictionary is based on. Still, you may also hear it followed by a bi-imperfect verb (an imperfect verb with the بـ prefix) even in Beirut, and it may even be the more common style in certain other areas of the Levant.

وعم (pronoun + وعم + imperfect verb) **while** بتحكي هي وعم تاكل. She talks while she eats.

عم NOUN (PLURAL: عموم)

(paternal) uncle الشركة اللي بيشتغل فيا لعمو. The company that he works for is his uncle's.

عمة NOUN

(paternal) aunt عمة جاد صغيرة. Jad's aunt is young.

عمتو NOUN (NO PLURAL), FEMININE

(paternal) auntie عمتو، عطيني المعلقة. Auntie, give me the spoon.

عمر NOUN (PLURAL: أعمار)

age قديش عمرك؟ How old are you?

- Notice how the vowel in the final syllable is elided (disappears) when a suffix beginning in a vowel is added (as in the example sentence 3úmur → 3úmrak). This is a common feature of Levantine Arabic.

عمر VERB (IMPERFECT: يعمر)

build لح يعمروا بناية جديدة هون. They're going to build a new building here.

عمل VERB (IMPERFECT: يعمل)

do شو بتعمل بوقت الفراغ؟ What do you do in your free time? **make** الصبي عمل رسمة لإمو. The boy made a drawing for his mom. عمل حالو **act, behave** بيعمل حالو غبي أوقات. He acts stupid sometimes.

عملة معدنية NOUN

coin ترك كم عملة معدنية عالطاولة. He left some coins on the table.

عمول معروف INTERJECTION

please عمول معروف، ساعدني! Please, help me!

عميق ADJECTIVE (ELATIVE: أعمق)

deep المسبح عميق. The pool is deep.

عن PREPOSITION

about الفيلم بيحكي عن حياتو الخاصة. The movie is about his private life. عن جديد **again** إتصل عن جديد. Call again.

87 | Beginning Learner's Levantine Arabic Dictionary

عن جد ADVERB (ALSO SPELLED: **عنجد**)

really. عنجد حب الفيلم He really liked the movie.

عند PREPOSITION

by, at. حط الرسالة عند الباب He put the letter by the door.
in one's country, where one is from. كتير شوب بالصيف عندكن؟ Is it very hot in the summer where you're from?
عندو PSEUDO-VERB **have** عندو إمتحان بكرا. He has an examination tomorrow.; رامي عندو إمتحان بكرا Rami has an examination tomorrow.

- When used as the pseudo-verb meaning 'have,' عند is always followed by a pronoun suffix. A noun precedes it, as in the second example above.

عنزة NOUN

goat. ما بحب حليب العنزة I don't like goat milk.

عنوان NOUN (PLURAL: عناوين)

title. ما في إتذكر عنوان الكتاب I can't remember the book's title.
address. لح إكتبلك عنواني I'll write down my address for you.

عنى VERB (IMPERFECT: يعني)

mean. شو بتعني هيدي الكلمة؟ What does this word mean?

عودة NOUN (NO PLURAL)

return. بنتطر بالبيت عودة ولادي من المدرسة. I wait at home for the return of my kids from school.

عوينات PLURAL NOUN

glasses. بيلبس عوينات لشوف أحسن. She wears glasses to see better.

عيد NOUN (PLURAL: أعياد)

holiday. بسافر بالعيد. I'm traveling on the holiday.
عيد ميلاد NOUN (PLURAL: أعياد ميلاد) **birthday** أيمتى عيد ميلادك؟ When is your birthday?

عيط VERB (IMPERFECT: يعيط)

shout, yell كان لازم نعيط لأن الموسيقى كانت عالية. We had to shout because the music was loud.; الولاد بيحبوا يعيطوا لمن يلعبوا. Kids like to yell when they play.

عيلة NOUN (PLURAL: عيل)

family. عزم عيلتو عالعشا He invited his family to dinner.

عين NOUN, FEMININE (PLURAL: عيون)

eye. عيونا عم يرعوها. Her eyes are itching her.

غ ـغـ ـغ
isolated / initial / medial / final

Ghayn is the nineteenth letter of the Arabic alphabet. It is the voiced equivalent of the letter خ *x* and has no equivalent in English. It is pronounced like the guttural r of French and German. Phonemic transcription: **ɣ**

ا ب ت ث ج ح خ د ذ ر ز س ش ص ض ط ظ ع غ ف ق ك ل م ن ه و ي

غابة NOUN

forest. النار دمرت الغابة. The fire destroyed the forest.

غاتو NOUN (PLURAL: غاتويات)

cake. هيدا الغاتو كتير طيب! This cake is delicious!

- This word has the regular plural suffix ات, but because it ends in a vowel, a buffer consonant is inserted: يات.
- غ is used to represent the hard *g* sound (as in English gas) in foreign words.

غارسون NOUN (PLURAL: غارسونية)

waiter. ما شفت الغارسون لنص ساعة. I haven't seen our waiter for half an hour.

- This is borrowed from the French word garçon, and while the French word may be outdated in French, it is still commonly used and considered respectful in Levantine Arabic.

غارسونة NOUN

waitress. شتغلت غارسونة لخمس سنين. I worked as a waitress for five years.

- As with most nouns referring to people, including jobs and nationalities, ة is added when referring to a woman.

غالي ADJECTIVE (ELATIVE: أغلى)

expensive. الخاتم غالي. The ring is expensive.

غامق ADJECTIVE (ELATIVE: أغمق)

dark. لابس قميص أحمر غامق. He's wearing a dark red shirt.

غبرة NOUN (NO PLURAL)

dust. كان في كتير غبرة عالكتب. There was a lot of dust on the books.

89 | Beginning Learner's Levantine Arabic Dictionary

غبي ADJECTIVE (PLURAL: **أغبيا**)
stupid, silly. بيعمل حالو غبي أوقات
He acts stupid sometimes.

غدا NOUN (PLURAL: **غداوات**)
lunch. باكل غدايي بالشغل
I eat my lunch at work.

غرب NOUN (NO PLURAL)
west. الهوا جايي من الغرب The wind is coming from the west.

غرفة NOUN (PLURAL: **غرف**)
room. دهنت الغرفة زهر I painted the room pink.
(PLURAL: **غرف سفرة**) **غرفة سفرة** dining room. ما بياكلوا بغرفة السفرة They don't eat in the dining room.
غرفة نوم (PLURAL: **غرف نوم**) bedroom سارة عم تفتش ع شقة فيا غرفة نوم وحدة. Sarah is looking for an apartment with one bedroom.

غرق VERB (IMPERFECT: **يغرق**)
drown. الصبي غرق بالنهر The boy drowned in the river.
be inundated. المدينة غرقت من الفيضان. The city was inundated in the flood.

غريب ADJECTIVE (ELATIVE: **أغرب**)
strange. منعيش بعالم غريب We live in a very strange world.

غزال NOUN (PLURAL: **غزلان**)
deer. شفت غزال بالغابة I saw a deer in the forest.

غسل VERB (IMPERFECT: **يغسل**)
wash. غسل التفاحة قبل ما ياكلا He washed the apple before eating it.

غش VERB (IMPERFECT: **يغش**)
deceive, con. غشني بالمنتج He deceived me about the product.

غطى VERB (IMPERFECT: **يغطي**)
cover. النسوان بيغطوا شعرن بالجامع. Women cover their hair in the mosque.
block. البناية الجديدة غطت المنظر. The new building blocked the view.

غلط ADJECTIVE, INVARIABLE
wrong. جوابك غلط! Your answer is wrong!
bad. التلفزيون غلط للأطفال. Television is bad for children.

غلطة NOUN (PLURAL: **أغلاط**)
mistake. تعلم من أغلاطو He learned from his mistakes.

غلى VERB (IMPERFECT: **يغلي**)
boil. الشاي عم يغلي The tea is boiling.

غني ADJECTIVE (ELATIVE: **أغنى**, PLURAL: **أغنيا**)
rich. الناس الأغنيا لازم يساعدوا الفقرا Rich people should help the poor.

غنى VERB (IMPERFECT: يغني)
sing. بتحب تغني She loves to sing.

غنية NOUN (PLURAL: أغاني)
song. شو غنيتك المفضلة؟ What is your favorite song?

غيتار NOUN
guitar. إبني بيلعب غيتار. My son plays the guitar.

- غ is pronounced as a hard *g* in this word (➲ See note for غاتو).

غير DETERMINER
(+ plural noun) other بحب إتعلم غير لغات. I like to learn other languages.

(+ singular noun) another عطيني غير قياس من هيدا الفستان. Give me another size of this dress.

غير VERB (IMPERFECT: يغير)
change. غير تيابو بعد النادي. He changed his clothes after the gym.

غيمة NOUN (PLURAL: غيوم)
cloud. ما في غيمة بالسما. There isn't a cloud in the sky.

Faa is the twentieth letter of the Arabic alphabet. It is pronounced f (as in the word fox). It also represents v in foreign words, in which case it may be written with three dots: ڤ Phonemic transcription: *f*

ا ب ت ث ج ح خ د ذ ر ز س ش ص ض ط ظ ع غ **ف** ق ك ل م ن ه و ي

ف CONJUNCTION (ALSO SPELLED: فا, فـ)
so, therefore لقط الطابة، ف ربح. He caught the ball, so he won.

فات VERB (IMPERFECT: يفوت)
enter فتحت الباب لفوت عالبيت. I opened the door to enter the house.

فاجأ VERB (IMPERFECT: يفاجئ)
surprise فاجأوها لعيد ميلادا. They surprised her for her birthday.

فإذا CONJUNCTION
so, therefore لقط الطابة، فإذا ربح. He caught the ball, so he won.

فاصل NOUN (PLURAL: فواصل)
break التلفزيون لح يحط الفيلم بعد الفاصل. The TV [channel] will put the movie after the break.

فاصوليا COLLECTIVE NOUN, FEMININE
beans ماما طبخت فاصوليا باللحمة. Mom cooked beans with meat.

فاضي ADJECTIVE (ELATIVE: أفضى)
empty العلبة فاضية. The box is empty.

فاق VERB (IMPERFECT: يفيق)
wake up, get up بتفيق دايما بكير. She always wakes up early.

فاكهة NOUN (PLURAL: فواكه)
fruit إمي شترت تفاح وغير فواكه. My mother bought apples and other fruit.

فتح VERB (IMPERFECT: يفتح)
open فتح الشباك. He opened the window.

فترة NOUN
(time) period. هيدي فترة صعبة. This is a difficult period.

فتش VERB (IMPERFECT: يفتش)
search, look (for) فتشت منيح بس ما لقيت مفاتيحي. I searched well but didn't find my keys.

فحص NOUN (PLURAL: فحوصات)
exam(ination), test الفحص بالمدرسة كان هين. The examination at school was easy.
(medical) test, analysis ناطر نتايج الفحص. I'm waiting for the test results.

فراغ NOUN
blank, emptiness كتبي إسمك بالفراغ. Write your name in the blank.
free time وقت الفراغ شو بتعمل بوقت الفراغ؟ What do you do in your free time?

فرجى VERB (IMPERFECT: يفرجي)
show فرجتني فستانا الجديد. She showed me her new dress.

فرد NOUN (PLURAL: فرودة)
gun البوليس عندو فرد. The police officer has a gun.

فرز VERB (IMPERFECT: يفرز)
freeze فرز الدجاج. He froze the chicken.

فرش NOUN (NO PLURAL)
furniture ستي شترت فرش جديد. My grandma bought new furniture.

فرشاية NOUN (PLURAL: فراشي)
brush في إستعمل فرشايتك؟ Can I use your brush?

فرشى VERB (IMPERFECT: يفرشي)
brush فرشى سنانو. He brushed his teeth.

فرصة NOUN (PLURAL: فرص)
chance عطيتو فرصة تانية. I gave him a second chance.
break التلاميذ بياخدو فرصة لياكلوا. The students take a break to eat.
vacation أنا عنجد بحاجة لفرصة! I really need a vacation!

فرض NOUN (PLURAL: فروض)
homework, assignment ما عندو ولا فرض بكرا. He doesn't have any homework for tomorrow.

فرع NOUN (PLURAL: فروع)
branch البنك عندو فروع بكل مدينة. The bank has branches in every city.

فرن NOUN (PLURAL: أفران)
oven نسيت الكيك بالفرن. She forgot the cake in the oven.
bakery, café روح شتري شوية خبز من الفرن. Go buy some bread from the bakery.

فرنسا NOUN (NO PLURAL)

بدّي زور فرنسا السنة الجاية. France
I want to visit France next year.

فريق (فرق: PLURAL) NOUN

هيدا الفريق كتير قوي. team This team is very strong.

فستان (فساتين: PLURAL) NOUN

لبست فستان أسود. She wore a dress black dress.

يفشل (IMPERFECT) VERB

فشل لأنّو ما درس. He failed fail because he didn't study.

فصل (فصول: PLURAL) NOUN

الكتاب فيه خمس فصول. section, chapter The book has five chapters.
في أربع فصول. There are season four seasons.
بيموت بنهاية الفصل act (theater) الأول. He dies at the end of the first act.

فضا NOUN (NO PLURAL)

رحلة الفضا كانت ناجحة. (outer)space The space trip was successful.

فضّة (فضيّات: PLURAL) NOUN

ما بشتري فضّة. silver I don't buy silver.

يفضّي (IMPERFECT) VERB

فضّت جزدانا عالطاولة. empty (out) She emptied her bag out on the table.

فطور NOUN

الفندق بيقدم فطور بالغرفة. breakfast The hotel serves breakfast in the room.

فقير (فقرا: PLURAL, أفقر: ELATIVE) ADJECTIVE

عيلتو كانت كتير فقيرة و poor (money) ما معا مصاري. His family was very poor and had no money.
أفكارو كتير poor, not good (quality) فقيرة. His ideas aren't very good.

يفكّر (IMPERFECT) VERB

عم فكر سافر الأسبوع الجايي. think I'm thinking of traveling next week.; بشو عم تفكر؟ What are you thinking about?

فكرة (أفكار: PLURAL) NOUN

ميرنا عندا كتير أفكار جديدة. idea Mirna has many new ideas.

يفلّ (IMPERFECT) VERB

لازم فلّ بكير. leave I should leave early.

فلسطيني (فلسطينية: PLURAL) NOUN, ADJECTIVE

في كتير فلسطينية بلبنان. Palestinian There are a lot of Palestinians in Lebanon.

⮕ See note for لبناني.

فنّ (فنون: PLURAL) NOUN

مريم بتتعلم الفنون الجميلة بإيطاليا. art Mariam is studying fine arts in Italy.

فِنْجان NOUN (PLURAL: فَناجين)
cup. عطيني فنجان قهوة. Give me a cup of coffee.

فُنْدُق NOUN (PLURAL: فَنادِق)
hotel. الفندق أربع نجوم. The hotel is four stars.

فِهِم VERB (IMPERFECT: يِفْهَم)
understand. ما بفهم عربي. I don't understand Arabic.

فَوَّت VERB (IMPERFECT: يْفَوِّت)
miss. التلميذ فوت المدرسة اليوم. The student missed school today.

فوتبول NOUN (NO PLURAL)
soccer. حضرت مباراة الفوتبول. I watched the soccer game.

فَوق
PREPOSITION **above** علقت الصورة فوق الكنباية. She hung the picture above the sofa.
PREPOSITION **over** الطيارة عم تطير فوق المحيط. The plane is flying over the ocean.
ADVERB **up** طلع لفوق! شو هيدا اللي فوق؟ Look up! What is that up there [in the sky]?
ADVERB **upstairs** إمك فوق. Your mother is upstairs.

في PSEUDO-VERB
there is, there are في فيلم حلو عالتي في. There is a nice movie on TV.
كان في there was, there were كان في عاصفة مبارح. There was a storm yesterday.

فَيّ NOUN
shade. بحب إقعد بالفي. I like to sit in the shade.

فَيَضان NOUN
flood. الشتي تسبب بفيضان. The rainfall caused a flood.

فاق VERB (IMPERFECT: يْفيق)
wake up. إما فيقتا بكير. Her mother woke her up early.

فيل NOUN (PLURAL: فِيَلة)
elephant. الفيل عندو دينين كبار. The elephant has big ears.

فيلم NOUN (PLURAL: أفلام)
movie, film. الفيلم مش للأطفال. The movie is not for kids.

فيو PSEUDO-VERB
can, is/are able to فيو يرقص كتير منيح. He can dance very well.

WE	فيي / فيني	–	فينا
YOU M.	فيك	YOU PL.	فيكن
YOU F.	فيكي		

95 | Beginning Learner's Levantine Arabic Dictionary

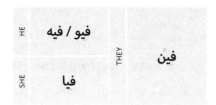

فيو كان could, was/were able to

كان فيا تركض بسرعة. She could run very fast.

- Notice that there are two variants for 'I can' and 'he can.' Both are common in Beirut and can be found in examples throughout the dictionary.

- Literally, في is the preposition 'in,' so you will occasionally see it used, as in the table, with pronoun suffixes (but rarely with nouns). (➲ See the example sentence for ثقة and the first note for وحدة.)

ق ق ق ق
isolated / initial / medial / final

Qaaf is the twenty-first letter of the Arabic alphabet. In Levantine Arabic, it is always a glottal stop–the same sound represented by the letter ء (hamza), as the sound between the vowels in uh-oh! or the Cockney pronunciation of be**tt**er–but never the *q* of Modern Standard Arabic. Phonemic transcription: **ʔ**

ا ب ت ث ج ح خ د ذ ر ز س ش ص ض ط ظ ع غ ف **ق** ك ل م ن ه و ي

قابل VERB (IMPERFECT: يقابل) **meet**. قابلتو لأول مرة بحفلة. I met him for the first time at a party.

قاتل VERB (IMPERFECT: يقاتل) **fight**. قاتل لحقوقو. He fought for his rights.

قادر PSEUDO-VERB, ADJECTIVE (FEMININE: قادرة, PLURAL: قادرين) **able, can**. هيدا الإستاذ قادر يساعد تلاميذو. This teacher can help his students.; هيدي الإستاذة قادرة تساعد تلاميذا. This teacher can help her students.

- This is the active participle of the verb قدر (be able to). It is used more or less interchangeably with the conjugated verb (➲ See قدر). As active participles are adjectives, they have three forms: masculine, feminine, and plural.

- In Arabic, agreement in gender and number is important. Notice, in the example sentences, the masculine and feminine forms of the demonstrative pronoun ('this'), قادر, the verb, and the pronoun suffix at the end. They all agree with the gender of the teacher.

قارة NOUN **continent**. في سبع قارات. There are seven continents.

قارن VERB (IMPERFECT: يقارن) **compare**. قارنت الأسعار بالمحلين. She compared the prices in the two shops.

- Note, in the example, that 'two' isn't expressed with a number but with the suffix ـين.

قاس VERB (IMPERFECT: يقيس)
measure. قاست إبنا She measured her son.

قاصص VERB (IMPERFECT: يقاصص)
punish. المعلمة قاصصت التلميذ. The teacher punished the student.

قاعة NOUN
hall. الصف بآخر القاعة The classroom is at the end of the hall.

قاعدة NOUN (PLURAL: قواعد)
rule. بعرف قواعد اللعبة I know the rules of the game.

قال VERB (IMPERFECT: يقول)
say. قال إنو ما بدو ياكل He said that he doesn't want to eat.
قال لـ say to, tell. ما قالتلي شو السبب الحقيقي. She didn't tell me what the real reason was.

- When the indirect object is a pronoun suffix, لـ is suffixed to the verb and can sometimes affect the verb's pronunciation. For example, يقول *biʔūl* (he says) + ـلي *-li* (to me) → بيقلي *biʔílli* (he says to me).

tell, speak. قلت الحقيقة I told the truth.

قاموس NOUN (PLURAL: قواميس)
dictionary. شتريت قاموس العربي الشامي. I bought a Levantine Arabic dictionary.

قانون NOUN (PLURAL: قوانين)
law. القوانين واضحين The laws are clear.
rule. بعرف قوانين اللعبة I know the rules of the game.

قبر NOUN (PLURAL: قبور)
grave. ما بيحب يزور القبور He doesn't like to visit graves.

قبض VERB (IMPERFECT: يقبض)
earn. بتقبض كتير بشغلا الجديد. She earns a lot at her new job.

قبل PREPOSITION
before. نقلنا لهون قبل الحرب We moved here before the war.
قبل هيك ADVERB before that. فيك تلعب برا، بس قبل هيك عمول فرضك. You can play outside, but before that, do your homework.
قبل ما CONJUNCTION before. قبل ما روح عالشغل، بشرب قهوة. Before I go to work, I drink coffee.

قبل VERB (IMPERFECT: يقبل)
(+ imperfect verb) agree. قبل يساعدني بتنضيف البيت. He agreed to help me clean the house.

قتل VERB (IMPERFECT: يقتل)
kill. هو كتير منيح ما فيه حتى يقتل نملة. He is so nice he can't even kill an ant.

قد بعض ADJECTIVE, INVARIABLE (ALSO SPELLED: **أد بعض**)

equal. المربع عندو جهات قد بعض. A square has equal sides.

- Literally, this expression means 'as much as each other.'
- Because ق is pronounced as a glottal stop in Levantine Arabic, some people may write hamza (ء) instead.

قدام PREPOSITION

in front of. صف قدام البيت. He parked in front of the house.

قدر VERB (IMPERFECT: **يقدر**)

(+ imperfect verb) **be able to, can**. غسان بيقدر يرفع أوزان تقيلة. Ghassan can lift heavy weights.; كانت بتقدر ترقص كتير منيح. She used to be able to dance very well.

قدرة NOUN (PLURAL: **قدرات**)

ability. التلميذ عندو قدرات مميزة. The student has special abilities.

- Notice how the sukuun (ْ) becomes damma (ُ) in the plural of this word. This is common for words which end in two adjacent consonants followed by ة and take the regular plural suffix ات.

قدم VERB (IMPERFECT: **يقدم**)

offer. قدملي شغل جديد. He offered me a new job.; المطعم قدملو عشا مجاني. The restaurant offered him a free dinner.

قدي ADVERB (ALSO: **قديش**)

how much. قدي حق هالفستان؟ How much does this dress cost?

قديم ADJECTIVE (ELATIVE: **أقدم**)

old. هيدا البيت قديم. This house is old.

قرا VERB (IMPERFECT: **يقرا**)

read. قرا كتاب جديد. He read a new book.

قرار NOUN

decision. كان قرار صعب. It was a difficult decision.

قرد NOUN (PLURAL: **قرود**)

monkey. القرد كان معلق ع شجرة. The monkey was hanging from a tree.

قرر VERB (IMPERFECT: **يقرر**)

decide. لازم تقرر بسرعة. You need to decide quickly.

قرن NOUN (PLURAL: **قرون**)

century. المدينة تغيرت عبر القرون. The city changed over the centuries.

قريب ADJECTIVE (ELATIVE: **أقرب**)

close. الطفل بيوقف قريب من إمو. The child stands close to his mother.

قرايب (PLURAL: **قرايبين**) cousin NOUN

قريبي بيعيش برا My cousin lives abroad.

قريبا ADVERB

بشوفك قريبا! soon See you soon!

قسم VERB (IMPERFECT: **يقسم**)

الإستاذ قسم التلاميذ لمجموعات. divide The teacher divided the students into groups.

قص VERB (IMPERFECT: **يقص**)

قصت شعرا. cut She cut her hair.

قصة NOUN (PLURAL: **قصص**)

ما بصدق هالقصة الغريبة! story, tale I don't believe this strange story!

القصة صعبة. matter, issue The matter is difficult.

قصد VERB (IMPERFECT: **يقصد**)

ما قصد يجرحا. He mean, intend didn't mean to hurt her.

قصر NOUN (PLURAL: **قصور**)

هيدا القصر كتير قديم. castle, palace This castle is very old.

قصير ADVERB (ELATIVE: **أقصر**, PLURAL: **قصار**)

لبست تنورة قصيرة. She wore a short skirt.

قضى VERB (IMPERFECT: **يقضي**)

قضيت نهاري عم بقرا. spend, pass I spent my day reading.

- If you only learn the meaning of this word in isolation, you won't be able to form a sentence using it correctly. You need to know the structure (pattern) used with it. Even when a structure isn't explicitly presented to you, you can analyze example sentences to find them. Let's take a look at the above example. In English, the pattern is 'spend' + time expression + gerund (-ing verb). And in Arabic? It is قضى + time expression + عم + (bi-)imperfect verb.

قطع VERB (IMPERFECT: **يقطع**)

الولاد ما لازم يقطعوا الشارع cross لحالن. Children should not cross the street alone.

قطع VERB (IMPERFECT: **يقطع**)

الطباخ قطع الدجاجة. cut The cook cut the chicken.

قطعة NOUN (PLURAL: **قطع**)

أكلت قطعة بيتزا. I ate a piece, slice slice of pizza.

قعد VERB (IMPERFECT: **يقعد**)

قعد جنبي. He sat next to me. sit

قفل NOUN (PLURAL: **قفول**)

حطيت المفتاح بالقفل. I put the lock key in the lock.

قفل VERB (IMPERFECT: **يقفل**)

قفل الباب. He locked the door. lock

100 | Beginning Learner's Levantine Arabic Dictionary

قلب NOUN (PLURAL: قلوب)
heart. عندا قلب طيب She has a good heart.

قلل VERB (IMPERFECT: يقلل)
lower, decrease. المحل قلل أسعارو. The store lowered its prices.

قلم NOUN (PLURAL: قلام)
pen المعلمة صلحت الإمتحانات بقلم أحمر. The teacher corrected the examinations with a red pen.
(PLURAL: قلام رصاص) قلم رصاص pencil. التلميذ كتب بقلم رصاص. The student wrote with a pencil.

قمر NOUN (PLURAL: أقمار)
moon. في شوف القمر بالسما بالليل. I can see the moon in the sky at night.

قميص NOUN (PLURAL: قمصان)
shirt. القميص كتير صغير. The shirt is very small.

قنينة NOUN (PLURAL: قناني)
bottle بحب إشرب بالكباية، مش بالقنينة. I like to drink from a cup, not a bottle.

قهوة NOUN (PLURAL: قهاوي)
coffee. بشرب قهوة الصبح I drink coffee in the morning.
café قهوة ع يروحوا بيحبوا الختيارية الحي. Old people like to go to the neighborhood café.

قوص VERB (IMPERFECT: يقوص)
(gun) shoot, fire. البوليس قوص بالهوا. The police fired in the air.

قوي ADJECTIVE (ELATIVE: أقوا, PLURAL: قوايا)
strong النسوان القوايا بيقدروا يعملوا أي شي. Strong women can do anything.

قياس NOUN
size عندك قياس أصغر من هيدا البنطلون؟ Do you have these pants in a smaller size?
measurement المسطرة عطت قياس غلط. The ruler gave a wrong measurement.

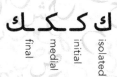

Kaaf is the twenty-second letter of the Arabic alphabet. It is pronounced k (as in the word <u>k</u>eep). Phonemic transcription: **k**

ا ب ت ث ج ح خ د ذ ر ز س ش ص ض ط ظ ع غ ف ق **ك** ل م ن ه و ي

كـ PARTICLE

as بيشتغل كإستاذ. He works as a teacher.

- This prefix is considered a particle and not a preposition because it would not take a pronoun suffix: not كنا but كنحنا (as we (do), as us)

ك PRONOUN, MASCULINE

(possessive) **your** شو إسمك؟ What is your name?
(object) **you** شفتك مبارح بالحي. I saw you yesterday in the neighborhood.

- Following a consonant, this suffix is pronounced -ak; after a vowel, it is -k.
- ⊃ See note for إنت.
- ⊃ See ي for a table of all pronoun suffixes.

ك PRONOUN, FEMININE

(possessive) **your** وين إختك؟ Where is your sister?
(object) **you** بحبك! I love you!

- ⊃ See note for إنت.
- ⊃ See ي for a table of all pronoun suffixes.

كارت NOUN (PLURAL: كروتة)

card عطى كروتة للمعازيم. He gave cards to the invitees.

كاسة NOUN

bowl بشرب الشوربة بالكاسة. I drink the soup in a bowl.

كاسكيت NOUN

cap لبس كاسكيت ليحمي حالو من الشمس. He wore a cap to protect himself from the sun.

كافيه NOUN

café كافيه ع يروحوا بيحبوا الختيارية الحي. Old people like to go to the neighborhood café.

كامل ADJECTIVE (ELATIVE: **أكمل**)

complete كامل لقت الفيلم على الإنترنت. She found the complete movie on the internet.

كاميرا NOUN, FEMININE

camera كاميرا جديدة. اشترى He bought a new camera.

كان VERB

be. كان رفيقي بالمدرسة. He was my friend at school.; كون منيح معو. Be nice to him.; بدا تكون إستاذة متل إما. She wants to be a teacher like her mother.; هو لبناني. He is Lebanese.; بنتي بالمدرسة. My daughter is at school.

- Notice that the verb كان is actually unexpressed in the last two example sentences. In Arabic, a subject without a verb is understood to include 'am/is/are.'

كانون الأول NOUN (NO PLURAL)

December. خلقت بكانون الأول. I was born in December.

كانون التاني NOUN (NO PLURAL)

January. رحلتي بكانون التاني. My trip is in January.

كب VERB (IMPERFECT: **يكب**)

spill. الغارسونة كبت القهوة ع جزداني. The waitress spilled coffee on my bag.

throw away, pour out هول ما تكب الوراق، مهمين! Don't throw out those papers! They're important!

كباية NOUN

(drinking) glass. الصبي شرب كباية مي. The boy drank a glass of water.

كبر VERB (IMPERFECT: **يكبر**)

grow, get bigger الولاد بيكبروا كل شهر. Children grow every month.

كبس VERB (IMPERFECT: **يكبس**)

press. كبس الكبسة ليفتح الباب. He pressed the button to open the door.

كبسة NOUN

button ضوي التلفزيون بالكبسة الخضرا! Turn on the TV with the green button!

كبير ADJECTIVE (ELATIVE: **أكبر**, PLURAL: **كبار**)

big, large منعيش بهيداك البيت الكبير عالتلة. We live in that big house on the hill.

كتاب NOUN (PLURAL: **كتب**)

book. هيدا كتابي المفضل. This is my favorite book.

كتب VERB (IMPERFECT: يكتب)
write كتب رسالة طويلة لخطيبتو. He wrote a long letter to his fiancée.
type في إكتب بسرعة عالكمبيوتر. I can type fast on the computer.

كتشف VERB (IMPERFECT: يكتشف)
discover مين كتشف الكهربا؟ Who discovered electricity?

كتف NOUN (PLURAL: كتاف)
shoulder عورت كتفي. I hurt my shoulder.

كتير (ELATIVE: أكتر)
DETERMINER (+ plural noun) a lot of, many في كتير ناس بالساحة. There are a lot of people in the square.
DETERMINER (+ singular noun) a lot of, much لازم تشرب كتير مي. You should drink a lot of water.
ADVERB (+ adjective) very, quite الطقس كتير بارد. The weather is very cold.
ADVERB (+ adjective) so عيونك كتير خضر. Your eyes are so green!
ADVERB (verb +) a lot, very much بتحكي كتير. She talks too much.; بحبك كتير. I love you very much.
⊃ See also أكتر.

كدشة NOUN
bite فيني آخد كدشة؟ Can I have a bite?

كذا DETERMINER
(+ singular noun) several بحب كذا كتاب. I like several books.

كذب VERB (IMPERFECT: يكذب)
lie, tell a lie (to) كذبت ع أهلا. She lied to her parents.

كذبة NOUN
lie ما تصدق كذبتو. Don't believe his lie.

كرر VERB (IMPERFECT: يكرر)
repeat كررت نفس الجملة. She repeated the same sentence.

كرسة NOUN (ALSO SPELLED: كرسي) (PLURAL: كراسي)
chair المطعم عندو كراسي عاليين للأطفال. The restaurant has highchairs for children.

كرمال هيك ADVERB
therefore, so شتت، كرمال هيك بقيت بالبيت. It rained, so I stayed at home.

كره¹ VERB (IMPERFECT: يكره)
hate بكره الموسيقى العالية. I hate loud music.

كره² NOUN
hate الكره إحساس مش حلو. Hate is not a nice feeling.

كزدر VERB (IMPERFECT: يكزدر)

roam. كزدرت البسينة بالشوارع The cat roamed the streets.

كسر VERB (IMPERFECT: يكسر)

break. كسرت عويناتا لما وقعت She broke her glasses when she fell.

كسول ADJECTIVE (ALSO: كسلان) (ELATIVE: أكسل)

lazy. هو ذكي بس كسول He is smart but lazy.

كعب NOUN (PLURAL: كعوب)

bottom. الحبلة وقعت بكعب البير The rope fell to the bottom of the well.

كفى VERB (IMPERFECT: يكفي)

be enough. الدوا بيكفي لأسبوع The medicine is enough for one week. continue. بس رجع من الشغل، كفى الفيلم When he returned from work, he continued the movie. complete. ما خلص رسمتو، ضل بالصف ليكفيا He didn't finish his drawing. He stayed in class to complete it.

كل DETERMINER

(+ definite plural noun) all كل التلاميذ عم يسمعوا معلمتن All of the students are listening to the teacher.; كل قرايبيني بأميركا All of my cousins are in America. (+ indefinite singular noun) each, every كل طفل بيحب إمو Every child loves his mother.

كل واحد (ALSO: الكل) everyone, everybody. كل واحد بدو يكون مبسوط Everybody wants to be happy. كل شي everything. بدي أعرف كل شي I want to know everything.

كلاس ADJECTIVE, INVARIABLE

classy, fancy, refined, high-class. المطعم كلاس This restaurant is fancy.

كلب NOUN (PLURAL: كلاب)

dog. عندي كلب إسمو فلافي I have a dog named Fluffy.

كلسات NOUN

(pair of) socks. لبست كلسات أبيض I put on a pair of white socks. فردة كلسات sock لقيت فردة كلسات تحت التخت I found a sock under the chair.

⊃ See note for جزمة

كلّف VERB (IMPERFECT: يكلّف)

cost. البيت بيكلف كتير مصاري A house costs a lot of money.

كلمة NOUN

word. كم كلمة بتعرف بالعربي؟ How many words do you know in Arabic?

كم DETERMINER

(+ singular noun) a few, some. في كم فرض ما عملن There are a few assignments he didn't do. كم تلميذ certain (+ singular noun) بيتصرفوا غلط. Certain students behave badly.

- Although كم requires a singular noun grammatically (as do numbers above 10 in Arabic), the noun requires plural agreement, as can be seen in the above examples (ن- 'them' in the first example and a verb conjugated for هن ('they') in the second example).

كمان ADVERB

also, too, as well يوسف مهمل بالمدرسة وبالبيت كمان. Youssef is careless at school and at home, too. عندي كمان تنين. I have two **more**.

كمبيوتر NOUN

computer جدي ما بيستغمل الكمبيوتر. My grandfather doesn't use a computer.

كمش VERB (IMPERFECT: يكمش)

catch كمشت سمكة. I caught a fish.; الشرطة كمشت الحرامية. The police caught the thieves.; كموش الطابة! Catch the ball!

كمل VERB (IMPERFECT: يكمل)

complete ما خلص رسمتو، ضل بالصف ليكملا. He didn't finish his drawing. He stayed in class to complete it.

كمية NOUN

amount شترى كمية بضاعة كبيرة. He bought a large amount of merchandise.

كن PRONOUN, PLURAL

(possessive) **your** واو! هيدا بيتكن؟ Wow! Is this your house? (object) **you** خليني عرفكن ع رفيقي الجديد. Let me introduce you to my new friend.

⊃ See note for إنت.

⊃ See ي for a table of all pronoun suffixes.

كنباية NOUN

sofa, couch قعدت عالكنباية. I sat on the sofa.

كنيسة NOUN (PLURAL: كنايس)

church كل العيلة بتروح عالكنيسة إيام الأحد. The whole family goes to church on Sundays.

كهربا NOUN, FEMININE (PLURAL: كهارب)

electricity الكهربا راحت عن جديد. The electricity went out again.

كوى VERB (IMPERFECT: يكوي)

iron كوى تيابو. He ironed his clothes.

كيس NOUN (PLURAL: كياس)

bag لازم نخفف إستعمال كياس البلاستيك. We should decrease the use of plastic bags.

كيف ADVERB

how كيفك؟ How are you?

كيك NOUN

cake هيدا الكيك كتير طيب! This cake is delicious!

isolated
initial
medial
final

Laam is the twenty-third letter of the Arabic alphabet. It is pronounced as the light L in the English word <u>l</u>eak—and not as the dark L in word du<u>ll</u>. Phonemic transcription: *l*

ا ب ت ث ج ح خ د ذ ر ز س ش ص ض ط ظ ع غ ف ق ك **ل** م ن ه و ي

لِ[1] PREPOSITION

for شترى هدية لإمو. He bought a gift for his mother.
to شو قلت للمرا؟ What did you say to the woman?
into قسمت البيتزا لشقف. I divided the pizza into pieces.
until قريت كتاب للساعة عشرة. I read a book until 10 o'clock.

- ل can also be *suffixed* onto a verb when it takes a pronoun suffix. كتبلي *kátabli* (he wrote to me). If the verb ends in ت (the first-person singular and masculine second-person singular perfect suffix), the ل is pronounced doubled (written with shadda): كتبت *katábit* (I/you wrote) → كتبتلا *katabtílla* (I/you wrote to her).

لِ[2] CONJUNCTION (ALSO: تَـ)

(+ imperfect verb) **in order to, to, so that** لازم يدرس ليجيب علامات منيحة. He should study to get good grades.

لأ INTERJECTION

no لأ، ما بدي قهوة. No, I don't want coffee.

لا... ولا CONJUNCTION

neither... nor... لا جدي ولا ستي بالبيت. Neither my grandfather nor my grandmother is home.

لاحظ (IMPERFECT: يلاحظ) VERB

notice ما لاحظ الكنباية الجديدة. He didn't notice the new sofa.

لازم

ADJECTIVE **necessary, required** عندي

كل الأدوات اللازمة لإبني علبة. I have all the necessary tools to build a box.
PSEUDO-VERB, INVARIABLE (+ imperfect verb)
must, have to, should, need to أنت مريض، لازم تروح عالمستشفى. You're sick. You have to go to the hospital.؛ لازم إشتري شي من المحل. I need to buy something at the store.؛ لازم تسمع كلمتي أحسنلك! You should listen to me better!

ما لازم (+ imperfect verb) **shouldn't** ما لازم تاكل قبل ما تروح عالتخت. You should not eat before you go to bed.

لازم ما (+ imperfect verb) **mustn't** لازم ما تعمل هيك! خطر! You mustn't do that! It's dangerous!

- لازم ما and ما لازم are interchangeable, but the latter has more emphasis.

لأن CONJUNCTION
because الصبي تعبان لأنو مريض. The boy is tired because he is ill.

WE	لأنا	—	لأني
YOU PL.	لأنكن	YOU M.	لأنك
		YOU F.	لأنك
THEY	لأنن	HE	لأنو
		SHE	لأنا

- If the clause following this conjunction does not have a noun subject, a pronoun suffix is added, as shown in the table and example sentence.

لايحة NOUN (PLURAL: لوايح)
list الإستاذ عندو لايحة بأسماء التلاميذ. The teacher has a list with the name of students.

لبس VERB (IMPERFECT: يلبس)
(without object) **get dressed** لبس ليروح عالحفلة. He got dressed to go to the party.
put on لبست جاكيتا. She put on her jacket.
wear بيلبس دايما دجينز مع قميص. He always wears jeans with his shirt.

لابس (FEMININE: لابسة, PLURAL: لابسين)
(active participle) **be wearing** لابس قميص أحمر غامق. He's wearing a dark red shirt.

لبق لـ VERB (IMPERFECT: يلبق)
suit, be fitting البنطلون لابقلو. The pants fit him.

لبنان NOUN (NO PLURAL), MASCULINE
Lebanon نحنا من جنوب لبنان. We are from the south of Lebanon.

- Most countries are grammatically feminine in Arabic. However, لبنان is an exception, as it is masculine. But what does the grammatical gender of a country matter?

> Words such as verbs and adjectives must agree with their noun. For example, مصر كبيرة (Egypt is big.) takes a feminine adjective, while لبنان حلو (Lebanon is beautiful.) requires a masculine adjective.

لبناني NOUN, ADJECTIVE

Lebanese. بتحب الأكل اللبناني؟ Do you like Lebanese food?

اللبنانية PLURAL (ALSO: الشّعب اللبْناني)

Lebanese people, the Lebanese. اللبنانية بيعيشوا حول العالم. Lebanese live all over the world.

لتقى VERB (IMPERFECT: يلتقي)

meet. لتقيت فيه لأول مرة بحفلة. I met him for the first time at a party.

لتنين PRONOUN

both. لتنين مرضى. Both of them are ill.

لح PARTICLE (ALSO: رح)

(+ imperfect verb) will. لح إحكيك بعدين. I will talk to you later.

لحالو ADVERB

alone, by oneself. رامي عايش لحالو. Rami lives alone.

لحد PREPOSITION

until. قريت كتاب لحد الساعة عشرة. I read a book until 10 o'clock.

لحد ما CONJUNCTION until. قريت كتاب

لحد ما مرتي إجت عالبيت. I read a book until my wife came home.

لحق VERB (IMPERFECT: يلحق)

chase. الكلب لحق البسينة. The dog chased the cat.

لحمة NOUN (PLURAL: لحوم)

meat. ما بتاكل لحمة. She doesn't eat meat.

لحية NOUN

beard. تغير شكلو بس شال لحيتو. His look changed when he removed his beard.

لطيف ADJECTIVE (PLURAL: لطفا)

kind, nice. قريبي كتير لطيف. My cousin is very kind.

لعب VERB (IMPERFECT: يلعب)

play. ما لازم تلعب بالنار. You should not play with fire.

لعبة NOUN (PLURAL: ألعاب)

game. اللعبة كتير سهلة. The game is very easy.
toy. البنت كسرت ألعابا. The girl broke her toys.
doll. البنت الصغيرة عم تلعب باللعبة. The little girl is playing with her doll.

- The word لعبة can refer to anything you play with and encompasses the meanings of the English words game, toy, and doll.

لعدة PREPOSITION

for (duration). سافرت لعدة إيام.
I traveled for many days.

لغة NOUN

language. بحكي تلات لغات. I speak three languages.

لف VERB (IMPERFECT: يلفّ)

turn. لف شمال عالزاوية. Turn left at the corner.

لقب NOUN (PLURAL: ألقاب)

nickname. سوسو لقبي. إسمي الحقيقي سحر. Sousou is my nickname. My real name is Sahar.

لقط VERB (IMPERFECT: يلقط)

catch. لقطت سمكة. I caught a fish.; لقوط الطابة! Catch the ball!

لقمة NOUN

bite. فيني آخد لقمة؟ Can I have a bite?

لقى VERB (ALSO: لاقى) (IMPERFECT: يلاقي)

find. لقت مفاتيحا تحت الكرسة. She found her keys under the chair.

لمّ VERB (IMPERFECT: يلمّ)

pick up, collect. الولد لمّ ألعابو. The child picked up his toys.

لما CONJUNCTION (ALSO: لمن)

when. أكلت العشا لما رجعت عالبيت. I ate dinner when I got home.
as. لما كنت رايح، رن التلفون. As I was leaving, the phone rang.

لمبة NOUN

lamp. ستعملت لمبة لضوي الأوضة. I used a lamp to light up the room.

لمع VERB (IMPERFECT: يلمع)

shine. عيونا بيلمعوا لما تشوفو. Her eyes shine when she sees him.

لو CONJUNCTION

if. لو الطقس كان منيح، كان راح عالبحر. If the weather were good, he would have gone to the beach.

لو سمحت (FEMININE: لو سمحتي) **excuse me**. لو سمحتي، كيف بوصل ع شارع الحمرا؟ Excuse me, how do I get to Al-Hamra Street?

ولو إنو **though, although, even though**. بحب إتعلم عربي، ولو إنو صعب. I like learning Arabic, even though it is difficult.

لوث VERB (IMPERFECT: يلوث)

pollute. المصنع عم يلوث المدينة. The factory is polluting the city.

لوح NOUN (PLURAL: لوح)

board. المعلمة كتبت الفرض عاللوح. The teacher wrote the homework on the board.

لوحة NOUN

painting. في كتير لوحات بالمتحف. There are many paintings in the museum.

111 | Beginning Learner's Levantine Arabic Dictionary

لوحدو ADVERB (ALSO: وحدو)

I	لوحدي	WE	لوحدنا
YOU M.	لوحدك	YOU PL	لوحدكن
YOU F.	لوحدك		
HE	لوحدو	THEY	لوحدن
SHE	لوحدا		

alone, by oneself. رامي عايش لوحدو. Rami lives alone.

لون NOUN (PLURAL: ألوان)

color. شو لونك المفضل؟ What is your favorite color?

لون VERB (IMPERFECT: يلون)

color. الأطفال لونوا الصورة. The children colored the pictures.

اللي PRONOUN (ALSO: يلي)

that, who, which هيدا الولد اللي ضرب البسينة! This is the boy who hit the cat!

- This word is casually pronounced *lli*.

ليستة NOUN

list. الإستاذ عندو ليستة بأسماء التلاميذ. The teacher has a list with the name of students.

ليل NOUN (ALSO: ليلة) (PLURAL: ليالي)

night. هي ما بتنام منيح بالليل. She doesn't sleep well at night.
tonight الليلة. رايحين عالسينما الليلة. We're going to the cinema tonight.
last night ليلة مبارح. ما قدرت نام ليلة مبارح. I couldn't sleep last night.

ليمون NOUN

orange. الليمون فاكهتي المفضلة. Orange is my favorite food.

- It sounds like 'lemon,' but it really does mean 'orange'! 'Lemon' is حامد.

ليه ADVERB (ALSO: ليش)

why ليه عملت هيك؟ Why did you do that?

Miim is the twenty-fourth letter of the Arabic alphabet. It is pronounced m (as in the word <u>m</u>an). Phonemic transcription: *m*

ا ب ت ث ج ح خ د ذ ر ز س ش ص ض ط ظ ع غ ف ق ك ل **م** ن ه و ي

ما PARTICLE

do(es) not ما بحبو. I don't like it.

did not ما رحنا عالسينما. We didn't go to the movies.

will not, is/are not going to ما رح تكتب رسالة. She isn't going to write a letter.

(+ pseudo-verb) **not**

ما عندو **not have** ما عندي سيارة. I don't have a car.

ما بدّو **not want** ما بدا تروح معنا. She doesn't want to go with us.

ما في **there is/are not** ما في كتير ناس بتفكر هيك. There aren't many people who think that way.

- ما is a negative particle. Notice that it precedes verbs and pseudo-verbs. Compare its usage to another negative particle, مش

مات VERB (IMPERFECT: يموت)

die كيف مات الكلب؟ How did the dog die?

مأخر ADJECTIVE

late وصل مأخر عالشغل. He arrived late at work.

مؤخراً ADVERB

lately الطقس حلو مؤخراً. The weather has been nice lately.

- Notice that the present perfect tense ('has been') is used in English with the adverb 'lately.' In Arabic, the present tense is used, so the above example sentence is literally 'The weather [is] nice lately.'

مادة NOUN (PLURAL: مواد)

material, substance البيت تعمر بمواد منيحة. The house was built with good materials.

subject موادي المفضلين كانوا العلوم والتاريخ بالمدرسة. Science and history were my favorite subjects in school.

ماشي

ADJECTIVE **working, in order** التلفون مش ماشي لأن ما في إرسال. The telephone is not working because there is no signal.

INTERJECTION **okay, all right** ماشي، لح إجي بكرا! Okay, I will come tomorrow!

ماشي حالو

ADJECTIVE, INVARIABLE*

okay, all right, fine الرسالة ماشي حالا. The letter is fine.

- ماشي is invariable, but حالو changes to agree with the subject.

ماضي

NOUN **past** إنسَ الماضي! Forget the past!

ADJECTIVE **last** عيد ميلادو كان الأسبوع الماضي. His birthday was last week.

مأكد

ADJECTIVE **certain** أنا مأكد إنو الصبح، تطلعت عالساعة. I am certain it is morning; I looked at the clock.

مألوف

ADJECTIVE **common** زواج القرايب مألوف بالعالم العربي. Marriage between cousins is common in Arab countries.

- You can see lots of words beginning with مـ on the following pages. Why so many? مـ is a common prefix in Arabic. It is used to create adjectives (active and passive participles) from verbs, as well as nouns denoting places. Take a look at some of the notes on the following pages. And if you try to look up a word that starts with مـ but can't find it, try removing the مـ and looking up the word. You might find the verb it is derived from and be able to work out its meaning.

ماما

NOUN (NO PLURAL), FEMININE

mom ماما، بدك ساعدك بالمطبخ؟ Mom, do you want me to help you in the kitchen?

مباراة

NOUN, FEMININE (PLURAL: مباريات)

(sport) **game, match** ربحوا مباراة الرياضة. They won the game.

➲ See note for حياة.

مبارح

ADVERB

yesterday شو عملت مبارح؟ What did you do yesterday?

last night ليلة مبارح (ALSO: مسا مبارح) ما قدرت نام ليلة مبارح. I couldn't sleep last night.

مبسوط ADJECTIVE

happy, glad أنا مبسوط لأن حبيت هديتك. I'm happy that you liked your gift.

- This word is related to the word نبسط, which shares a similar concept. We say that they are related because they share the same root, that is, three consonant–in this case, the root is ب س ط.

مبين ADJECTIVE

looking, appearing مبينة تعبانة. She looks tired.

- You may notice several that begin in مـ and have a shadda (ّ) over the second to last consonant. These are either active or passive participles of measure-II verbs and act as adjectives or nouns derived from their verbs.

متأني ADJECTIVE

careful هو متأني بفرضو. He is careful with his homework.

متحف NOUN (PLURAL: متاحف)

museum التلاميذ فين يزوروا المتحف ببلاش. Students can visit the museum for free.

مترو NOUN

subway ما عنا مترو بلبنان. We don't have a subway in Lebanon.

متساوي ADJECTIVE

equal المربع عندو جهات متساوية. A square has equal sides.
even كل واحد ربح اللعبة مرتين، فإذا كلن متساويين. Everyone won the game twice, so they are all even.

متل PREPOSITION

like, as ما في حدا متلك. There is no one like you.; بدو يكون إستاذ متل بيو. He wants to be a teacher like his father.
متل العادة ADVERB as usual سمير رجع تعبان من الشغل متل العادة. Samir came back from work tired as usual.
متل ما CONJUNCTION as النتيجة كانت متل ما توقعت. The result was as I expected.

متلك VERB (IMPERFECT: يمتلك)

hold بيمتلك حصة بالشركة. He holds a stake in the company.

مثل VERB (IMPERFECT: يمثل)

act مثل بكتير أفلام. He acted in many movies.

مثلا ADVERB

for example فيك ترسم مثلا عصفور. You can draw, for example, a bird.

مجانا ADVERB

(for) free المطعم بيعطي مشروب مجانا مع الأكل. The restaurant gives drinks for free with food.

- You may notice a few words that end in ا in the dictionary. This ending is pronounced -an, and most of these words are adverbs (but never nouns, adjectives, or verbs).

مَجاني ADJECTIVE

free بَس تِشتَري تنَين مُنتَج، الأرخَص مَجاني. When you buy two products, the cheaper one is free.

مُجَرَّد ADVERB

just, mere مُجَرَّد فِكرة السَّفَر بالطَّيّارة بتخَوِّفو. Just the idea of traveling by plane scares him.

مَجموع NOUN

total مَجموع حَقّ البضاعة غالي. The total cost of the products is expensive.

مَجموعة NOUN

group كُل مَجموعة فيا خَمس تلاميذ. Each group has five students.
collection في مَجموعة جديدة مِن التياب بالمَحَل. There is a new collection of clothes in the store.

- Notice that مَجموعة only differs from the noun مَجموع in its final ة, but because these words don't refer to people, it would be wrong to assume that مَجموعة is the feminine equivalent of مَجموع. They are related in meaning, but have different uses.

مَجنون ADJECTIVE (PLURAL: مَجانين)

crazy, insane هِيّ مَجنونة بِبسيناتا. She is crazy about her cats.

- Remember that adjectives have to agree with the noun or pronoun they are describing in gender and number. In the above example, notice that the adjective has the feminine suffix ة.

مَحاية NOUN

eraser التِّلميذ صَحَّح الغَلطة بالمَحاية. The student corrected the mistake with an eraser.

مُحِبّ ADJECTIVE

friendly الغارسون مُحِبّ. The waiter is friendly.

مُحبَط ADVERB

depressed, down, blue مبارَح كُنت حاسِس حالي مُحبَط. Yesterday I was feeling down.

مُحتَرَم ADJECTIVE

respected, esteemed الإستاذ كتير مُحتَرَم. The teacher is very respected.

مَحَطّة NOUN

(radio) station فيك تغَيِّر مَحَطّة الراديو؟ Can you change the radio station?
(bus, train) station أخَدت تاكسي للمَحَطّة الرَّئيسية. I took a taxi to the

main station. نطرت بالمحطة لساعة. (bus) **stop**
I waited at the (bus) stop for an hour.

محل NOUN

place في كتير محلات مشوقة للزيارة بلبنان. There are a lot of interesting places to visit in Lebanon.

بشوفو بكل محل. كل محل ADVERB **everywhere**
I see him everywhere.

شي محل ADVERB **somewhere, anywhere** شايفك بشي محل بس ما بتذكر وين. I've seen you somewhere, but I don't remember where.

محلو ADVERB **in one's place, instead of one** عملت الفرض محلي. She did the homework in my place.

store, shop شو شتريتوا من المحل؟ What did you buy from the shop?

- The words مكان and مطرح are synonyms of this word in its first meaning, 'place,' and are interchangeable, but only محل has the second meaning of 'store/shop.'

محمّس ADJECTIVE

excited أنا محمّس بخصوص الشغل الجديد. I am excited about this new job.

محى VERB (IMPERFECT: يمحي)

erase الإستاذ محى اللوح. The teacher erased the board.

محيط NOUN

ocean المحيط أزرق. The ocean is blue.

مختلف ADJECTIVE

different رحنا ع مطعم مختلف مبارح. We went to a different restaurant yesterday.

مدام NOUN, FEMININE

Mrs. هيدا مقعد مدام فرح. This is Mrs. Farah's seat.

مدامة NOUN

wife (of __) مدامتو معلمة. His wife is a teacher.

- This noun is always in a possessive construction, followed by a pronoun suffix or noun. If you wanted to say 'a wife,' it would be a different word entirely: زوجة.

مدخل NOUN (PLURAL: مداخل)

entrance هيدا المدخل للزوار. This entrance is for the visitors.

- This word is derived from the verb دخل (enter), and has the prefix مـ to denote a place—a place you enter, that is, an entrance. You can find several more such words on the following pages—for instance, مدرسة, مكتب, مسبح, مزرعة, and مكان.

مدرسة NOUN (PLURAL: مدارس)
school. بيعيش جنب المدرسة He lives near the school.

- Can you tell which verb this word is derived from? Just remove its prefix and suffix to find its three-letter root.

مدور ADJECTIVE
round. الطاولة مدورة. The table is round.

مدينة NOUN (PLURAL: مدن)
city. أضوية المدينة بتلمع بالليل. The city lights shine at night.

مرا NOUN, FEMININE (ALSO SPELLED: مرة) (PLURAL: نسوان)
woman. هي مرا حلوة She's a pretty woman.; هوليك النسوان التنين بيشتغلوا مع بعض. Those two women work together.

مربع NOUN
square. الولد رسم مربع ومثلث ليرسم بيت. The boy drew a square and a triangle to make a house.

مربى NOUN
jam. بحب إدهن مربى عالخبزة. I like to spread jam on bread.

مرة NOUN
(occurrence) time. لح سامحك هالمرة! I'll forgive you this time!

مرة تانية ADVERB again. إتصل مرة تانية. Call again.

مرة ADVERB once. قابلتو مرة بحفلة. I met him once at a party.

مرتين ADVERB twice. رحت ع لبنان مرتين. I've been to Lebanon twice.

تلات مرات ADVERB three times. إختي حضرت هيدا الفيلم تلات مرات. My sister has seen this movie three times.

- As with other words denoting time (days of the week, months, etc.), مرة is technically a noun but is more often used as an adverb of time, as in the above examples.

مرة NOUN (PLURAL: نسوان)
(+ pronoun suffix or noun) wife (of). مرة جاد معلمة. Jad's wife is a teacher.; مرتو معلمة. His wife is a teacher.

- This word is actually a variant of the word مرا (woman) but is always followed by a pronoun suffix or noun. The plural is irregular: نسوان (their wives).

مرتب ADJECTIVE
tidy, organize. شوف كيف البيت مرتب! Look how tidy the house is!

مرتبة NOUN
place, rank. أخدت المرتبة الأولى. She got first place.

118 | Beginning Learner's Levantine Arabic Dictionary

مرحبا INTERJECTION

hello. قالت مرحبا لما شافتني She said hello when she saw me.

مرسي INTERJECTION

thanks, thank you. مرسي! إنت لطيف! Thanks! You're kind!

مرض VERB (IMPERFECT: يمرض)

get sick. مرض ف ضل بالبيت He got sick, so he stayed at home.

مرق VERB (IMPERFECT: يمرق)

pass. السيارة مرقت من قدام بيتي The car passed by my house.

مركز NOUN (PLURAL: مراكز)

center. رحنا عالمركز التجاري We went to the commercial center.

مركز الشرطة NOUN police station

مركز الشرطة عاليمين. The police station is on the right.

rank, position. مركزو بالشركة منيح His rank in the company is good.

مركزي ADJECTIVE

central. البنك المركزي بيسكر بالأعياد The central bank is closed on holidays.

- This is a nisba adjective, formed by adding ي to a noun: مركز (center) → مركزي (central). (⊃ See note for حقيقي)

مريح ADJECTIVE

comfortable. شتريت تخت مريح. I bought a comfortable bed.

مريض ADJECTIVE (PLURAL: مرضا)

ill, sick, unwell. ما رحت عالشغل لأني مريضة. I didn't go to work because I'm sick.

مزبوط ADJECTIVE (ALSO SPELLED: مظبوط) (ELATIVE: أزبط)

correct, right, true. جوابك مزبوط! Your answer is right!

مزحة NOUN

joke. مزحتو مش مهضومة His joke isn't funny.

- This word can be pronounced *máz-ha* in careful speech, but it more natural, relaxed speech, assimilation occurs, whereby the z sound becomes unvoiced when followed by an unvoiced consonant such as ح ḥ: *más-ha* (⊃ See notes for تزوج)

مزدوج ADJECTIVE

double, dual. عندي جنسية مزدوجة I have dual nationality.

مزرعة NOUN (PLURAL: مزارع)

farm. المزرعة فيا دجاج The farm has chickens.

مزوج ADVERB

(not odd) even. تنتين وأربعة هن أرقام مزوجة. Two and four are even numbers.

مس NOUN, FEMININE

miss. مسّ نور معلمتي Miss Nour is my teacher.

مسا NOUN (PLURAL: أمسيات)

evening
في المسا in the evening. لازم ما تاكل كتير المسا. You mustn't eat a lot in the evening
هالمسا this evening. بشوفك هالمسا. I'll see you this evening.
مسا مبارح yesterday evening, last night. ما قدرت نام مسا مبارح. I couldn't sleep last night.

مساحة NOUN

space, area. مشان مساحة أكتر، شال الكنباية. For more space, he removed the sofa.

مسار NOUN

path, course. مسارو ناجح. His path is successful.

مساعدة NOUN

help, support. بدي مساعدة لنقي تيابي. I need help choosing my clothes.

مسؤولية NOUN

responsibility, duty. الأهل عندن مسؤوليات تجاه ولادن. Parents have responsibilities toward their children.

مسبح NOUN (PLURAL: مسابح)

swimming pool. قضيت الصيفية جنب المسبح. I spent the summer by the swimming pool.

مستشفى NOUN (PLURAL: مستشفيات)

hospital. راحت عالمستشفى لأنا مريضة. She went to the hospital because she is sick.

مستقبل NOUN (NO PLURAL)

future. بدو يكون حكيم بالمستقبل. He wants to be a doctor in the future.

مستلشق ADJECTIVE

careless. بلال مستلشق بالمدرسة. Bilal is careless at school.

مستند NOUN

document. هيدا مستند مهم. This is an important document.

مستهتر ADJECTIVE

careless. بلال مستهتر بالمدرسة. Bilal is careless at school.

مسرحية NOUN

play. ممثل مشهور لح يشارك بالمسرحية. A famous actor will participate in the play.

مسطح ADJECTIVE

flat. كم شخص بيصدقوا الأرض مسطحة. Few people believe the earth is flat.

مسطرة NOUN (PLURAL: مساطر)

ruler. رسمت خط بـمسطرة. I drew a line with a ruler.

مسك VERB (IMPERFECT: يمسك)

hold. الطفل مسك إيد إمو. The child held his mother's hand.

مسمار NOUN (PLURAL: مسامير)

nail. علق الصورة بـمسمار. He hung the picture on a nail.

مسيو NOUN

mister, Mr. مسيو زياد جايي اليوم. Mr. Ziad is coming today.

- This word is borrowed from the French 'monsieur.' The spelling of borrowed words varies from person to person; people just try to capture the pronunciation as closely as possible using the Arabic script.

مش PARTICLE

مش am/is/are not (+ non-verb) هي مش مشكلتي! It is not my problem!; مش هون. She isn't here. (+ active participle) مش قادر روح عالشغل اليوم. I can't go to work today.

- مش is a negative particle used in equational sentences and with active participles. It is interchangeable with منو (⊃ See منو) but not with ما (⊃ See ما).

مشان PREPOSITION

for. شترت حليب مشان إبنا الصغير. She bought milk for her small son. مشان هيك، therefore, so شتت مشان هيك بقيت بالبيت. It rained, so I stayed at home.

مشروب NOUN

beverage, drink. المطعم بيقدم مشروبات مجانا. The restaurant offers drinks for free.

- This word is actually the past participle adjective of the verb شرب (⊃ See note for ممنوع), literally meaning 'drunk' but is also used as a noun to mean 'that which is drunk.'

مشط NOUN (PLURAL: مشاط)

brush, comb. عطيني المشط. Give me the brush.

مشط VERB (IMPERFECT: يمشط)

brush, comb. بتحب تمشط شعر بنتا. She likes to brush her daughter's hair.

مشغول ADJECTIVE

busy. بيي دايما مشغول. My father is always busy.

مشكل NOUN (PLURAL: مشاكل)

fight. كسر منخارو بالمشكل. He broke his nose in the fight.

مشكلة NOUN (PLURAL: **مشاكل**)
problem, trouble جدي عندو مشاكل صحة. My grandfather has health problems.

مشمس ADJECTIVE
sunny الطقس مشمس اليوم. The weather is sunny today.

مشهد NOUN (PLURAL: **مشاهد**)
(theater) **scene** بكيت لمن شافت المشهد الحزين. She cried when she saw the sad scene.

مشهور PLURAL: **مشاهير**)
ADJECTIVE (ELATIVE: **أشهر**) **famous** المطعم مشهور لأكلو. The restaurant is famous for its food.
ADJECTIVE (ELATIVE: **أشهر**) **popular** هيدي الغنية مشهورة. This song is popular.
NOUN **celebrity, star** هو واحد من أكبر المشاهير بلبنان. He's one of the biggest celebrities in Lebanon.

مشوق ADJECTIVE
interesting الكتاب كتير مشوق. The book is very interesting.

مشي VERB (IMPERFECT: **يمشي**)
walk لح إمشي عالبيت. I'm going to walk home.

مصاري PLURAL NOUN
money البيت بيكلف كتير مصاري. A house costs a lot of money.

مصرياتو one's money حطّيت مصرياتي بالبانك. I put my money in the bank.

- This word has a unique form when followed by a pronoun suffix or noun: **مصاري** (money) → **مصريات الرجال** (the man's money).
- This word has an interesting etymology. It is related to the word **مصر** (Egypt), and is actually the plural of the now obsolete **مصرية**, an Egyptian coin which was used in the Levantine region for a time during Ottoman and/or British rule.

مصر NOUN, FEMININE
Egypt زرت مصر السنة الماضية. I visited Egypt last year.

مصرف NOUN (PLURAL: **مصارف**)
bank نبيل حط مصرياتو بالمصرف. Nabil put his money in the bank.

مصلحة NOUN (PLURAL: **مصالح**)
business بلشوا مصلحة عائلية. They started a family business.

مصنع NOUN (PLURAL: **مصانع**)
factory جوزا بيشتغل بالمصنع. Her husband works at the factory.

مطابق ADJECTIVE
suitable, fitting أكل الكلاب مش مطابق للإنسان. Dog food is not fit for humans.

مطاط NOUN

rubber. هول الصبابيط معمولين من مطاط. These boots are made of rubber.

مطاطي ADJECTIVE

rubber-. الولد لعب بلعبة مطاطية. The child played with a rubber toy.

مطبخ NOUN (PLURAL: مطابخ)

kitchen. إمي دايما بالمطبخ. My mom is always in the kitchen.

مطرح NOUN (PLURAL: مطارح)

place. في كتير مطارح مشوقة للزيارة بلبنان. There are a lot of interesting places to visit in Lebanon.

كل مطرح ADVERB everywhere. بشوفو بكل مطرح. I see him everywhere.

شي مطرح ADVERB somewhere, anywhere. شايفك بشي مطرح بس ما بتذكر وين. I've seen you somewhere, but I don't remember where.

مطرحو ADVERB in one's place, instead of one. عملت الفرض مطرحي. She did the homework in my place.

مطرقة NOUN

hammer. في مطرقة بعلبة الأدوات. There is a hammer in his toolbox.

مطعم NOUN (PLURAL: مطاعم)

restaurant. في مطعم جديد حد بيتي. There is a new restaurant next to my house.

مطفي ADJECTIVE

off, turned off. التلفزيون مطفي. The television is off.

مطل NOUN

view. حجزت أوضة مع مطل. I booked a room with a view.

مطلوب ADJECTIVE

ADJECTIVE necessary, required. عندي كل الأدوات المطلوبة لإبني علبة. I have all the necessary tools to build a box.

مظهر NOUN (PLURAL: مظاهر)

appearance, look(s). مظهرا حلو. She looks nice. (lit. Her appearance is nice.)

مع PREPOSITION

with. بتعيش مع إما. She lives with her mother.; مين معي؟ (on the phone) Who am I speaking with? (lit. Who is with me?)

مع إنو CONJUNCTION although, even though. بدي إقعد برا، مع إنو الطقس مش حلو. I want to sit outside, even though the weather isn't nice.

مع بعض ADVERB together. بيعيشوا مع بعض. They live together.

مع السلامة INTERJECTION goodbye, bye. مع السلامة، بشوفك قريبا. Bye! See you soon!

معجون NOUN

clay, putty الولاد بيحبوا يلعبوا بالمعجون. Children like to play with putty.

معزوم NOUN (PLURAL: معازيم)

guest, invitee كان في كتير معازيم بالعرس. There were many guests at the wedding.

معصّب ADJECTIVE

angry أمين معصّب كتير. Amin is very angry.

معطف NOUN (PLURAL: معاطف)

coat خود المعطف. في برد برا. Take the coat. It's cold outside.

معظم DETERMINER

most معظم الولاد بيحبوا الشوكولاتة. Most kids love chocolate.

معقول ADJECTIVE

possible كل شي معقول إذا شتغلنا مع بعض. Everything is possible if we work together.

معلّق ADJECTIVE

hanging, hung up الصورة معلقة عالحيط. The picture is hanging on the wall.

معلّمة NOUN

(female) teacher المعلمة بتحب تلاميذا. The teacher loves her students.

- Although a masculine version of this word (معلّم) also exists, a male teacher is more commonly referred to as إستاذ (⊃ See إستاذ)

معلومة NOUN

information قريت هيدي المعلومة بالجريدة. I read this information in the newspaper.

معليش INTERJECTION

never mind نسيت شو بدي قول، معليش. I forgot what I want to say. Never mind!

excuse me, pardon, sorry معليش، فيني إستعمل قلمك؟ Sorry, can I use your pen?

معمل NOUN (PLURAL: معامل)

factory جوزا بيشتغل بالمعمل. Her husband works at the factory.

مغسلة NOUN (PLURAL: مغاسل)

sink المغسلة مليانة صحون. The sink is full of dishes.

مغيّم ADJECTIVE

cloudy مغيمة اليوم. It's cloudy today.

- In the example sentence, the adjective is feminine because the unexpressed but implied subject is دنيا (weather).

مفاجئ ADJECTIVE

sudden سمعت صوت مفاجئ. I heard a sudden noise.

مفتاح NOUN (PLURAL: مفاتيح)
key. ضيعت مفاتيحي. I lost my keys.

مفتوح ADJECTIVE
open. المحل الجديد فتح هيدا الأسبوع. The new store opened this week.

مفرش NOUN (PLURAL: مفارش)
cloth. حطي مفرش عالطاولة لتخليا نضيفة. Put a cloth on the table to keep it clean.

مفرق NOUN (PLURAL: مفارق)
(street) corner. ناطر عالمفرق. I'm waiting on the corner.

مفضّل ADJECTIVE
favorite. فاكهتي المفضلة هي التفاح. My favorite fruit is apples.

مفيد ADJECTIVE
useful. هول الأدوات كتير مفيدين. These tools are very useful.

مقابلة NOUN
interview. هيدا الممثل بيكره المقابلات. This actor hates interviews.

مقابيل PREPOSITION
across from, opposite. بتلاقي مركز الشرطة مقابيل الشارع. You can find the police station across the street.; قعدت مقابيلو. I sat opposite him.

مقص NOUN
scissors. قصيت الورقة بالمقص. I cut the paper with scissors.

مقعد NOUN (PLURAL: مقاعد)
seat. مقعدو جنبي. His seat is next to me.

مكان NOUN (PLURAL: أماكن)
place. في كتير أماكن مشوقة للزيارة بلبنان. There are a lot of interesting places to visit in Lebanon.
كل مكان ADVERB everywhere. بشوفو بكل مكان. I see him everywhere.
شي مكان ADVERB somewhere, anywhere. شايفك بشي مكان بس ما بتذكر وين. I've seen you somewhere, but I don't remember where.
مكانو ADVERB in one's place, instead of one. عملت الفرض مكاني. She did the homework in my place.

مكتب NOUN (PLURAL: مكاتب)
desk. قعد ع مكتبو ودور الكمبيوتر. He sat at his desk and turned on his computer.
office. مكتبو حد الصالة. His office is near the hall.

مكتبة NOUN
bookstore. شتريت هيدا الكتاب من المكتبة مبارح. I bought this book at the bookstore yesterday.
library. بيروح عالمكتبة مرة بالشهر. He goes to the library once a month.

مكسّرات PLURAL NOUN

crackers. شتريت مكسّرات للحفلة.
I bought crackers for the party.

مكنة NOUN

machine. شترى مكنة جديدة. He bought a new machine.

ملح NOUN (PLURAL: موالح)

salt. بليز، عطيني الملح. Please, give me the salt.

ملعقة NOUN (PLURAL: ملاعق)

spoon. بدي ملعقة للشوربة. I want a spoon for the soup.

ملك NOUN (PLURAL: ملوك)

king. الملك ختيار. The king is old.

ملكة NOUN

queen. الملكة كتير حلوة. The queen is very beautiful.

ملوث ADJECTIVE

polluted. البحر ملوث لأن الناس بيكبّوا بلاستيك فيه. The sea is polluted because people throw plastic in it.

ملوّن ADJECTIVE

colored. رسم ع ورق ملوّن. He drew on colored paper.

ملى VERB (IMPERFECT: يملي)

fill. ملى القنينة مي. He filled the bottle with water.

• This verb has two objects, whereas English would require the preposition 'with' before the second object.

مليان ADJECTIVE

full. وقتو مليان. His time is full.

مليون NUMBER (PLURAL: ملايين)

million. تمان مليون لبناني بيعيشوا برا لبنان. Eight million Lebanese live outside of Lebanon.

ممثل NOUN

actor. الممثل معروف. The actor is well known.

• In the example sentence, we see the word معروف (known), but it is not listed in the dictionary. Why? It is the passive participle of the verb عرف (know), the base form of this word. (➲ See note for ممنوع) It would not be practical to have entries for every passive participle (and the many other forms conjugated verbs take) in the dictionary, so if its translation is predictable (as in 'know' → 'known'), a past participle will not have its own entry.

ممر NOUN

path. هيدا الممر بيودي عالجنينة. This path leads to the garden.

ممكن ADJECTIVE

possible. كل شي ممكن إذا شتغلنا مع بعض. Everything is

126 | Beginning Learner's Levantine Arabic Dictionary

possible if we work together.
ADVERB **probably** البيبي عم يبكي عشان ممكن بدو حليب. The baby is crying because he probably wants milk.

ممل ADJECTIVE

boring رفقاتو مملين. His friends are boring.

ممنوع ADJECTIVE

forbidden ممنوع التدخين هون. It is forbidden to smoke here.

- This word is the passive participle of the measure-I verb منع (forbid). (A measure-I verb is a simple verb form that consists of three consonants. More on verb measures can be found on p. 115 of our book *Levantine Arabic Verbs*.) Past participles of measure-I verbs are formed by adding the prefix مـ, a sukuun (ْ) over the first consonant of the verb, and the long vowel و between the second and third consonants. You can find several entries in this dictionary that have the same pattern.

مميز ADJECTIVE

special, distinctive شترى هدية مميزة لإمو. He bought a special gift for his mother.

من PREPOSITION

from قرا إيميل من نورا. He read an email from Noura.

من ADVERB **where from** إنت من وين؟ Where are you from?

من فضلك INTERJECTION **please** من فضلك، ساعدني! Please, help me!

- كـ is the masculine singular pronoun suffix, so if you are addressing a woman, be sure to change the phrase to من فضلِك, and when speaking to more than one person: من فضلكن

من قبل ADVERB **before, previously, already** زرت بيروت من قبل؟ Have you been to Beirut before?
of الخاتم معمول من دهب. The ring is made of gold.
since ما شفتو من السنة الماضية. I have not seen him since last year.
ago بلشت سوق من سنتين. I started driving two years ago.
than أنا أكبر من إختي. I'm older than my sister.
because of أنا تعبان شوي من الشغل. I'm a bit tired because of work.

مناسب ADJECTIVE

suitable, appropriate, proper هيدا الفستان مش مناسب للعرس. This dress is not appropriate for the wedding.; هيدي اللعبة مناسبة لكل الأعمار. This game is suitable for all ages.

مناسبة NOUN

event, special occasion المدينة

منتج NOUN
product. المحل بيبيع منتجات قديمة. The store sells old products.

منتشر ADJECTIVE
spread out, widespread. المدارس الخاصة منتشرة بالمدينة. Private schools are spread throughout the city.

منخار NOUN (PLURAL: مناخير)
nose. كسرت منخارا. She broke her nose.

منصب NOUN (PLURAL: مناصب)
(job) position. منصبي بالشركة منيح. My position in the company is good.

منطقة NOUN (PLURAL: مناطق)
area. بيت جدي بمنطقة رايقة. My grandfather's house is in a quiet area.

منطو NOUN (PLURAL: منطويات)
coat. خود المنطو. في برد برا. Take the coat. It's cold outside.

- This word has the regular plural suffix ات, but because it ends in a vowel, a buffer consonant is inserted: يات.

منظر NOUN (PLURAL: مناظر)
view. حجزت أوضة مع منظر. I booked a room with a view.

يمنع VERB (IMPERFECT: يمنع)
prevent, forbid. منع الصحافة تسأل أسئلة. He forbid the press from asking questions.

منو (ALSO: مش)

	–	WE	
YOU M.	مني		منا
YOU F.	منك	YOU PL.	منكن
	منك		
HE	منو	THEY	منن
SHE	منا		

am/is/are not. مني مشغول. I'm not busy.

منيح ADJECTIVE (PLURAL: مناح)
good, nice, fine. بعرف مطعم منيح. I know a good restaurant.; الطقس منيح. The weather is nice.; أنا منيحة مدام، مرسي. I'm fine, ma'am. Thank you.

bad (مش مناح :PLURAL) مش منيح. التلفزيون مش منيح للأطفال. Television is bad for children.

- Instead of a separate word for 'bad,' people literally say 'not good.'

kind, nice. قريبي كتير منيح. My cousin is very kind.

ADVERB well. بتحكي عربي منيح! You

speak Arabic well!

- You might expect that this adjective would have the elative form أمنح (better, best), following the pattern of other elatives. But instead, the elative forms of less common synonyms (borrowed from Modern Standard Arabic) are used. (⮕ See أحسن, أزبط, and أفضل)

مهذّب ADJECTIVE
polite. رايان كتير مهذبة Rayan is very polite.

مهضوم ADJECTIVE
funny. كانت مزحة كتير مهضومة It was a really funny joke.

مهمّ ADJECTIVE (ELATIVE: أهمّ)
important. أخدت قرار مهم She made an important decision.

مهمل ADJECTIVE
careless. بلال مهمل بالمدرسة Bilal is careless at school.

موبايل NOUN
cell phone. نسيت موبايلي بالبيت. I forgot my cell phone at home.

مودل أزياء NOUN
fashion model. بتشتغل كمودل أزياء She works as a model.

موديرن ADJECTIVE, INVARIABLE
modern. شترت فرش موديرن She

bought modern furniture.

موز COLLECTIVE NOUN
bananas. السعادين بيحبوا الموز. Monkeys love bananas.

موسيقى NOUN (NO PLURAL), FEMININE
music. بيسمع موسيقى لما يعمل فرضو. He listens to music when he does his homework.

موضوع NOUN (PLURAL: مواضيع)
topic, subject, issue, matter. هيدا موضوع خاص، ما بدي إحكي عنو. This is a private matter. I don't want to talk about it.

موظّف NOUN
employee. هو الموظف الوحيد اللي بيوصل مأخر. He is the only employee who arrives late.

- This is a passive participle. Originally, it is an adjective meaning 'employed,' but, as with many adjectives, has taken on usage as a noun. Although the verb this passive participle is based on is not listed in this limited dictionary, by knowing about the formation of participles, you can work out that the verb for 'employ' would be وظف.

موف ADJECTIVE, INVARIABLE
purple. شتريت طقية موف. I bought a purple hat.

- موف is borrowed from the French mauve. Adjectives borrowed from other languages are normally invariable, which is why the adjective does not have the feminine ending ة here. (➲ See note for زهر)

موقع إلكتروني NOUN (PLURAL: مواقع إلكترونية)
website. الشركة عندا موقع إلكتروني. The company has a website.

موقف NOUN (PLURAL: مواقف)
parking lot. الموقف مليان سيارات. The parking lot is full of cars.

موهبة NOUN (PLURAL: مواهب)
skill, talent. عندو كتير مواهب. He has many skills.

مي NOUN, FEMININE (ALSO: ماي) (PLURAL: مياه)
water. فيك تعطيني شوية مي بليز؟ Could you give me some water, please?

ميت ADJECTIVE (PLURAL: أموات)
dead. هو ميت. He is dead.

مية NUMBER
hundred. عد للمية. Count to one hundred.

(ALSO SPELLED: ميت) (+ singular noun) hundred. الكتاب فيو مية صفحة. The book has a hundred pages.

ميلة NOUN
side. ضربت الميلة الشمال من سيارتي. I hit the left side of my car.

مين PRONOUN
who. مين تصل؟ Who called?

anyone, whoever. بيصدق مين ما كان. He believes anyone.

Nuun is the twenty-fifth letter of the Arabic alphabet. It is pronounced n (as in the word n<u>a</u>me). Phonemic transcription: *n*

ا ب ت ث ج ح خ د ذ ر ز س ش ص ض ط ظ ع غ ف ق ك ل م **ن** ه و ي

ـن PRONOUN, PLURAL

(possessive) **their** بيحبوا ولادن. They love their children.
(object) **them** لح تزورن اليوم؟ Will you visit them today?

- When ـن is added to a word ending in ي, this suffix pronoun pronounced *-yun*: خلي *xálli* (let) → خليّن *xallíyun* (let them). After other vowels, a buffer consonant is inserted: ـهن *-hun*: خلا *xálla* (he let) → خلاهن *xalláhun* (he let them).

➲ See ي for a table of all pronoun suffixes.

ـنا PRONOUN, PLURAL

(possessive) **our** بيتنا قديم. Our house is old.; هول جيرانا. These are our neighbors.

- Notice that the pronoun suffix ـنا is added to a noun ending in ن,

resulting in a double *n* sound. This is written with a shadda (ّ) over the ن rather than writing the consonant twice.

(object) **us** فيك تساعدنا؟ Can you help us?

➲ See ي for a table of all pronoun suffixes.

ناجح ADJECTIVE (ELATIVE: أنجح)

He is a هو رجال ناجح. **successful** successful man.

نادي NOUN (PLURAL: نوادي)

gym بيرفع أوزان بالنادي. He lifts weights in the gym.

نار NOUN, FEMININE (PLURAL: نيران)

fire الولاد كانوا عم يلعبوا بالنار. The children were playing with fire.

ناس PLURAL NOUN

people كتير ناس إجوا عالحفلة. Many

people came to the party.

ناسب VERB (IMPERFECT: يناسب)
fit, be suitable (for), be appropriate (for). البنطلون ناسبو The pants fit him.

ناشف ADJECTIVE (ELATIVE: أنشف)
dry, arid. البلد عندو طقس ناشف. The country has a dry climate.

ناصح ADJECTIVE (ELATIVE: أنصح)
fat. هو ناصح لأن بياكل كتير. He is fat because he eats a lot.

نام VERB (IMPERFECT: ينام)
sleep. ما بنام منيح بالليل. I don't sleep well at night.
go to sleep, go to bed. نمت مأخر مبارح. I went to bed late last night.

نبات NOUN
plants, greenery. عندي نبات بمكتبي. I have plants in my office.

نبسط بـ VERB (IMPERFECT: ينبسط)
enjoy. نبسط بالحفلة. He enjoyed the party.

- While the English verb 'enjoy' takes a direct object, the Arabic verb نبسط requires a preposition, بـ. Keep your eyes out for such verbs throughout the dictionary. There are several.

نبش VERB (IMPERFECT: ينبش)
search, look (for). نبشت منيح بس ما لقيت مفاتيحي. I searched hard but didn't find my keys.

نبيد NOUN
wine. صبيت كاسة نبيد. I poured a glass of wine.

نتبه VERB (IMPERFECT: ينتبه)
pay attention, be careful. نتبه عالطريق وسوق ع مهل. Be careful on the road and drive slowly.

نتج VERB (IMPERFECT: ينتج)
result. نجاحو نتج من شغلو المنيح. His success resulted from his good work.

نتفة ADVERB
a (little) bit. ذاكرة ستي ضعيفة نتفة. My grandmother's memory is a bit weak.

نتهى VERB (IMPERFECT: ينتهي)
end. الحرب نتهت. The war ended.

نتيجة NOUN (PLURAL: نتايج)
result. النتيجة كانت متل ما توقعت. The result was as I expected.
(school) grade. نتيجة التلميذ كانت منيحة. The student's grade was good.

نجاح NOUN
success. بتمنالك حياة مليانة نجاح! I wish you a life full of success!

نجح VERB (IMPERFECT: ينجح)
pass. نجح الإمتحان He passed the examination.

نجم NOUN (PLURAL: نجوم)
star, celebrity. هو واحد من أكبر النجوم بلبنان He's one of the biggest stars in Lebanon.
- A female star would be نجمة, formed by adding ة to the masculine noun. (➲ See note for صاحب)

نجمة NOUN (PLURAL: نجوم)
(celestial) star. فيك تعد كل النجوم اللي بالسما؟ Can you count all of the stars in the sky?
- Notice that the word for a literal, celestial star is pronounced نجمة while a female star/celebrity is نجمة.

نحاس NOUN
copper. الناس بيستعملوا النحاس من زمان People have been using copper for ages.

نحنا PRONOUN
we. نحنا كتير مبسوطين إنو شفناك We are very happy to see you.

نخفض VERB (IMPERFECT: ينخفض)
drop, fall, decrease. الحرارة نخفضت The temperature dropped.

نزف VERB (IMPERFECT: ينزف)
bleed. الصبي وقع عن بيسيكليتو ونزف The boy fell off his bike and was bleeding.

نزل VERB (IMPERFECT: ينزل)
drop, fall, decrease. الحرارة نزلت The temperature dropped.
get out, disembark. بنزل عالمفرق الجاي I'll get out at the next corner.

نسي VERB (IMPERFECT: ينسا)
forget. نسيت مفاتيحي بالبيت I forgot my keys at home.

نشاط NOUN (PLURAL: نشاطات, أنشطة)
activity. زادت الشركة نشاطاتا The company increased its activities.
- This noun has two common plurals: an irregular plural, as well as a regular plural formed with ـات.

نشر VERB (IMPERFECT: ينشر)
spread. نشرت الأخبار المنيحة She spread the good news.
publish. نشرنا هيدا القاموس لنساعدكن تتعلموا عربي We have published this dictionary to help you learn Arabic.

نشيط ADJECTIVE (ELATIVE: أنشط)
active. الصبيان نشيطين أكتر من البنات Boys are more active than girls.

نَصّ NOUN (PLURAL: نْصاص)
half. بعْنا نصّ بْضاعْتْنا. We sold half of our products.
middle. وْقِفْت بْنصّ الغُرْفة. I stood in the middle of the room.

نْضُر ADJECTIVE (ELATIVE: أنْضر)
bright, radiant. جِلْدا كْتير نْضُر. Her skin is absolutely radiant.

نضَّف VERB (IMPERFECT: يْنضِّف)
clean. الطَّبّاخ بِينضِّف إيديه قبْل ما يِطْبُخ. The chef cleans his hands before cooking.

نْضمّ لـ VERB (IMPERFECT: يِنْضمّ)
join. نْضمّيت لَلْمجْموعة. I joined the group.

نْضيف ADJECTIVE (ELATIVE: أنْضف, PLURAL: نْضاف)
clean. تْيابي نْضاف، ما تْغسْلينْ. My clothes are clean. Don't wash them.

نطّ VERB (IMPERFECT: يْنُطّ)
jump. الأطْفال بِيحِبّوا يْنُطّوا عالتَّخْت. Children like to jump on the bed.

- Unlike English, Arabic uses the definite article to express generalizations. 'Children' (in general) is الأطْفال (literally 'the children') in Arabic.

نطر VERB (IMPERFECT: يْنطُر)
wait (for). ما تْنطُرْني! Don't wait for me!

- Notice that this verb takes a direct object and does not require a preposition as the English verb 'wait' does.

نطْرة NOUN
wait. النَّطْرة كانت طْويلة ومُمِلّة. The wait was long and boring.

نفخ VERB (IMPERFECT: يِنْفُخ)
blow out. نفخْت الشُّموع. I blew out the candles.
blow up, inflate. الأب نفخ البالون لَبِنْتو. The father blew up the balloon for his daughter.
نفخ ع blow on. نفخ عالشّورْبة لَيْبرِّدا. He blew on the soup to cool it down.

نفْس الـ
the same. سألتْني نفْس السُّؤال مرّة تانْية. You asked me the same question again.
نفْس الشي the same thing. بسّ نفْس الشي! But it's the same thing!

نفض VERB (IMPERFECT: يِنْفُض)
dust. نفضْت الطّاوْلة قبْل العشا. She dusted the table before dinner.

نْفعل VERB (IMPERFECT: يِنْفعِل)
be excited, become agitated, get worked up. نْفعل بسّ سِمع الخبر. He got excited when he heard the news.

نقاش NOUN

discussion. فتحوا نقاش مهم. They opened an important discussion.

نقتل VERB (IMPERFECT: ينقتل)

be killed. رفيقو نقتل بالحرب. His friend was killed in the war.

- Measure-I verbs (⊃ See note for ممنوع) can generally be made passive by adding the prefix ن and have the same vowel pattern as this verb. These are known as measure-VII verbs. Only a few common measure-VII verbs are listed in this dictionary, but knowing this rule, you should be able to form more. For example, دفش (push) would become ندفش (be pushed).

نقطة NOUN (PLURAL: نقط)

point. حكينا عن نقطة مهمة. We talked about an important point. (punctuation) period, full stop. الجملة بتنتهي بنقطة. A sentence ends with a period. drop. الدكتور قالي حط نقطة دوا بكل دينة. The doctor told me to put one drop of medicine in each ear.

نقل VERB (IMPERFECT: ينقل)

move. نقلت ع بيت جديد. She moved to a new house.

نقى VERB (IMPERFECT: ينقي)

choose, select, pick. نقى هدية لمرتو. He chose a gift for his wife.

clear up. هيدا الدوا بينقي الجلد. This medication clears up the skin.

نكتب VERB (IMPERFECT: ينكتب)

be written. كتابو لح ينكتب بالإنجليزي. His book will be written in English.

نمل COLLECTIVE NOUN (SINGULAR: نملة)

ants. لقيت نمل حد علبة السكر. I found ants near the box of sugar.

نموذج NOUN (PLURAL: نماذج)

model, sample. رسم نموذج لبيت أحلامو. He drew a model of his dream house.

نمّى VERB (IMPERFECT: ينمّي)

develop, make grow. نمى موهبتو. He developed his skill.

نهار NOUN

day. قضيت نهاري عم بقرا. I spent my day reading.

نهاية NOUN

end. ما تقلي نهاية القصة. Don't tell me the end of the story!

نهر NOUN (PLURAL: أنهار)

river. بعيش جنب النهر. I live near the river.

نوع NOUN (PLURAL: أنواع)

type, kind, sort. أي نوع أفلام بتحب؟ What kind of movies do you like?

135 | Beginning Learner's Levantine Arabic Dictionary

نَوْم NOUN (NO PLURAL)

sleep. النوم المنيح مهمّ للصحّة.
Good sleep is important for health.

نيسان NOUN (NO PLURAL)

April. الجوّ حلو بنيسان.
The weather is nice in April.

ه ـهـ ـه ه
isolated / initial / medial / final

Haa is the twenty-sixth letter of the Arabic alphabet. As it is pronounced h (as in <u>h</u>ello), it is not a difficult sound for English speakers. However, it can pose more of a challenge when it occurs at the end of a word, as in the word كره *kirih* (hate). Phonemic transcription: **h**

ا ب ت ث ج ح خ د ذ ر ز س ش ص ض ط ظ ع غ ف ق ك ل م ن ه و ي

ـه PRONOUN, MASCULINE

(possessive) **his, its** غداه بياكل بالشغل. He eats his lunch at work.

(object) **him, it** بتزوريه؟ Do you visit him?

- This suffix is added to words ending in a vowel. The ه is can be silent or pronounced *h,* and it lengthens the preceding vowel sound. غدا *yáda* (lunch) → غداه *yadā(h)* (his lunch); بتزوري *bitzūri* (you f. visit) → بتزوريه *bitzūrī(h)* (you f. visit him (⊃ See also و)

- ⊃ See note for هو for the usage of pronouns for humans and non-humans.

- ⊃ See ي for a table of all pronoun suffixes.

هال DETERMINER

(+ noun) **this, these** هالبنت إختو.

This girl is his sister.; هالسيارات غالين. These cars are expensive.; هالرجال جارنا. This man is our neighbor.

- هال is actually ه prefixed to the definite article, so the ل can be assimilated (⊃ See notes for الـ). It is used with masculine, feminine, and plural nouns. It is interchangeable with هيدي, هيدا, and هول.

هاي INTERJECTION

hi هاي، كيفك؟ Hi, how are you?

هب VERB (IMPERFECT: يهب)

blow الهوا عم يهب. The wind is blowing.

هبط VERB (IMPERFECT: يهبط)

land الطيارة لح تهبط هلأ. The plane will land now.

هتمّ بـ (يهتمّ) VERB (IMPERFECT:)
care about, show concern for. بيهتمّ بمظهرو. He cares about his looks.
be interested in. كتير بهتمّ بالتاريخ. I'm very interested in history.

هجم ع (يهجم) VERB (IMPERFECT:)
attack. هجم الكلب عالبسينة. The dog attacked the cat.

هجوم NOUN
attack. الشرطة وقفت الهجوم. The police stopped the attack.

هجّى (يهجّي) VERB (IMPERFECT:)
spell. الولد تعلّم يهجّي إسمو بالمدرسة. The child learned to spell his name at school.

هديّة (هدايا) NOUN (PLURAL:)
gift, present. شتريت هدايا لإمي. I bought some gifts for my mother.

هرب (يهرب) VERB (IMPERFECT:)
escape. جرّب يهرب من الحبس. He tried to escape from prison.

هريبة NOUN
escape. الهريبة فشلت. The escape failed.

هزّ (يهزّ) VERB (IMPERFECT:)
shake. هزّ الدوا منيح. Shake the medicine well.
rock. الإم هزّت البيبي. The mother rocked the baby.

هلّأ ADVERB (ALSO SPELLED: هلق)
now. شو عم تعمل هلّأ؟ What are you doing now?

- Because the glottal stop sound can be represented by ق and hamza (ء) in Levantine Arabic, you may encounter variations in spelling.

همّ (هموم) NOUN (PLURAL:)
worry, concern. تسبّبت لإما بكتير همّ؟ She caused her mother much worry.

هنّ PRONOUN (ALSO SPELLED: هنّي)
they. هنّ بنفس الصفّ. They are in the same classroom.

هندسة NOUN
engineering. بيدرس هندسة. He studies engineering.

هو PRONOUN (ALSO SPELLED: هوّي)
he. هو يلي فتح الباب. He is the one who opened the door.
it

- As all nouns in Arabic are either masculine or feminine, there is no neutral pronoun 'it' for inanimate objects. Everything is either هو (he) or هي (she).

⮕ See note for أنا.

هوا (هوايات) NOUN (PLURAL:)
air. الهوا ملوّث بالمدن. The air is polluted in the cities.

في كتير هوا اليوم! There's a lot of wind today! wind

هواية NOUN

شو هواياتك؟ What are your hobbies? hobby

هول DETERMINER, PRONOUN, PLURAL

THIS M.	هيدا	THESE	هول
THIS F.	هيدي		
THAT M.	هيداك	THOSE	هوليك
THAT F.	هيديك		

هول التلاميذ رايقين. These students are calm.; هول السيارات غالين. These cars are expensive. these

- See note for هيدي.
- There are regional variations for demonstratives, such as هودي and هيدول for 'these.' In this dictionary, we just list the most widely used, "standard" forms.

هوليك DETERMINER, PRONOUN, PLURAL

الطاولة الجديدة مبيني حلوة مع هوليك الكراسي. The new table looks nice with those chairs.; عطيني هوليك الكتب، بليز! Give me those books, please! those

هون ADVERB

بعيش هون. I live here. here

هونيك ADVERB

فيك تلاقي مفاتيحك هونيك! You can find your keys there! there

هي PRONOUN (ALSO SPELLED: هيي)

هي عندا ولاد. She has children. she

- See note for هو.
- See note for أنا.

هيدا DETERMINER, PRONOUN, MASCULINE

هيدا الصبي قريبي. This boy is my cousin. this

هيداك DETERMINER, PRONOUN, MASCULINE

هيداك الرجال جاري. That man is my neighbor. that

هيدي F.

هيدي البنت إختو. This girl is his sister. DETERMINER this

هيدي كانت أول رحلة إلي برا. This was my first trip abroad. PRONOUN this (one)

- The Levantine Arabic demonstratives (equivalent to this/that/these/those) are labeled as determiners and pronouns. By determiner, it is meant that you can use it as part of a noun phrase. In this case, the noun takes the definite article, as in the first example above. However, demonstratives can also be used as pronouns (without a noun), as in the second example.

هَيْديك DETERMINER, PRONOUN, FEMININE

that هيديك المرا عمتي. That woman is my aunt.

هَيْك ADVERB

like this, thus ما شفت أبدا شي هيك. I have never seen anything like this.

هَيْكَل NOUN (PLURAL: هَياكل)

structure, framework هيكل البيت قوي. The frame of the house is strong.

أهْيَن ADJECTIVE (ELATIVE:)

simple, easy التمرين هين. The exercise is simple.

و

و ـو ـو ـو
isolated / initial / medial / final

Waaw is the twenty-seventh letter of the Arabic alphabet. When it precedes a vowel, it is pronounced w (as in <u>w</u>est): وَ *wa*, وِ *wi*, وُ *wu*, وا *wē*, وي *wī*. It is also w in diphthongs: ـو *aw*, ـِو *iw*. Otherwise, following a consonant, it is a long vowel: ـو *ō* (as in American English kn<u>ow</u>, but without the glide to w), as French <u>eau</u> or German <u>oh</u>; ـو *ū* (as in m<u>oo</u>n), but shorter at the end of a word.

ا ب ت ث ج ح خ د ذ ر ز س ش ص ض ط ظ ع غ ف ق ك ل م ن ه **و** ي

و CONJUNCTION

and غسان وريما بنفس الصف. Ghassan and Rima are in the same classroom.

- This word is commonly written without a space between it and the word following it, resembling a prefix. However, many people do tend to write it as a separate word.
- It is pronounced as a short *u* or *w*.

ـو PRONOUN, MASCULINE

(possessive) **his** هيدا مش بيتو. This isn't his house.
(object) **him** بتعرفو؟ Do you know him?

- This suffix is only added to words ending in a consonant. (⊃ See also ه)
- ⊃ See note for هو for the usage of pronouns for humans and non-humans.
- ⊃ See ي for a table of all pronoun suffixes.

واجب NOUN

obligation, duty واجبات الأهل عندن تجاه ولادن. Parents have obligations toward their children.

واجهة NOUN

front, façade واجهة المحل عندا شباك كبير. The front of the store has a big window.

واحد NUMBER (FEMININE: وحدة)

one السؤال رقم واحد هين. Question number one is easy.; بس بنت وحدة إجت عالحفلة. Only one girl came to the party.
single سافرت كتير مرات بسنة وحدة. I traveled many times in a single year.

141 | Beginning Learner's Levantine Arabic Dictionary

واسع ADJECTIVE (ELATIVE: أوسع)
wide. المحلّ عندو مجموعة واسعة. The store has a wide collection.

واضح ADJECTIVE (ELATIVE: أوضح)
clear. الأحرف بالكتاب واضحين. The letters in the book are clear.

واطي ADJECTIVE (ELATIVE: أوطى)
low. الشمس واطية المسا. The sun is low in the evening.

وافق VERB (IMPERFECT: يوافق)
وافق (+ imperfect verb) agree. ساعدني بتنضيف البيت. He agreed to help me clean the house.

وثق VERB (IMPERFECT: يوثق)
trust. ما بتوثق فيك؟ Doesn't she trust you?

- Studying example sentences can help you understand how to use words in context. Here, we can see that the verb requires a preposition before its object.

وج NOUN (PLURAL: وجوه)
face. وجو بيصير أحمر بعد التمرين. His face becomes red after exercise.
بوج PREPOSITION in front of. صف بوج البيت. He parked in front of the house.

وجبة NOUN
meal. لازم ناكل تلات وجبات باليوم. We should eat three meals a day.

وجع[1] VERB (IMPERFECT: يوجع)
hurt. سني بيوجعني لما إشرب مي باردة. My tooth hurts when I drink cold water.

وجع[2] NOUN (PLURAL: أوجاع)
pain. حاسس بوجع بإيدي الشمال. I feel pain in my left hand.

وجع VERB (IMPERFECT: يوجع)
hurt. سني بيوجعني لما إشرب مي باردة. My tooth hurts when I drink cold water.

وحدة NOUN
unit. كتاب التلاميذ فيو تمان وحدات. The students' book has eight units.

- فيو literally means 'in it.' (⟳ See the second note for فيو)

وحدة قياس unit of measurement. الوحدة القياس مش نفسا بكل البلاد. The unit of measurement is not the same in all countries.

- وحدة can also be the feminine form of واحد (one). (⟳ See واحد)

وحدو ADVERB (ALSO: لوحدو)

وحدنا	WE	وحدي	I
وحدك	YOU M.		
وحدكن	YOU PL.		
وحدك	YOU F.		

142 | Beginning Learner's Levantine Arabic Dictionary

HE	وحدو	
SHE	وحدا	THEY وحدن

alone, by oneself رامي عايش وحدو. Rami lives alone.

وحيد ADJECTIVE

lonely بحس حالي وحيد لما يروحوا رفقاتي. I feel lonely when my friends leave.

ودّع VERB (IMPERFECT: يودّع)

say goodbye, bid farewell ودّعت رفقاتي. I said goodbye to my friends.

ودّى VERB (IMPERFECT: يودّي)

lead, guide هو لح يوديك ع مقعدك. He will show you to your seat.

ورا PREPOSITION

behind خبت الكتاب ورا خزانة الكتب. She hid the book behind the bookcase.

وردة NOUN (PLURAL: ورود)

flower عطاها ورود ع عيد ميلادا. He gave her flowers for her birthday.

ورق COLLECTIVE NOUN (SINGULAR: ورقة, PLURAL: وراق)

paper رسم ع ورق ملون. He drew on colored paper.

ورقة piece of paper, sheet of paper كتب إسمو ع ورقة. He wrote his name

on a sheet. شتريت كم ورقة وقلم. I bought some paper and a pen.

ورق (شجر) leaves (tree) ورق الشجر أحمر وأصفر بالخريف. Leaves are red and yellow in the fall.

- We don't always need to add **شجر** if it is clear from context that you mean 'leaves' and not 'paper.'

ورق شدة playing cards بحب إلعب ورق شدة عالكمبيوتر. I like to play cards on the computer.

وزن NOUN (PLURAL: أوزان)

weight خسر وزن. He has lost weight.

وسخ ADJECTIVE (ELATIVE: أوسخ)

dirty وج الصبي كان وسخ. The boy's face was dirty.

وسط NOUN (PLURAL: أوساط)

middle وقفت بوسط الغرفة. I stood in the middle of the room.

وصل VERB (IMPERFECT: يوصل)

arrive (at), reach وصل الضيف بكير. The guest arrived early.; لمن وصلت عالمحل، كان مسكر. When I reached the shop, it had already closed.

وصل لـ receive, get لح يوصلا الرسالة بكرا. She will receive the letter tomorrow.

- This verb doesn't literally mean 'receive,' although it is used when we would say 'receive' in English. The subject and object are reversed from English, as it literally means 'arrive to,' as in 'The letter will arrive to her tomorrow.'

وصّى ع VERB (IMPERFECT: يوصي)
order. وصّت ع أكل She ordered some food.

وضع NOUN (PLURAL: أوضاع)
condition, state. وضع البيت مش منيح The house's condition is bad. situation. الوضع صعب The situation is difficult.

وطن NOUN (PLURAL: أوطان)
country, nation. بحب وطني I love my country.

وطّى VERB (IMPERFECT: يوطّي)
lower. وطّيت كرسة السيارة I lowered the car seat. (volume) turn down. فيك توطّي الراديو، عمول معروف Could you turn down the radio, please?

وظيفة NOUN (PLURAL: وظايف)
job. لقت وظيفة بشركة منيحة She found a job in a good company.

وعد NOUN (PLURAL: وعود)
promise. هي مبسوطة بسبب وعدو She is happy because of his promise.

وعد VERB (IMPERFECT: يوعد)
promise. وعد يزورني اليوم He promised to visit me today.

وعّى VERB (IMPERFECT: يوعّي)
wake up, make get up. إما وعّتا بكير Her mother woke her up early.

وفّر VERB (IMPERFECT: يوفّر)
save. وفّرت مصاري لتشتري سيارة She saved money to buy a car.

وقت NOUN (PLURAL: أوقات)
time. ما عندي وقت هلأ I don't have time right now.
أي وقت ADVERB anytime. فيك تزورني أي وقت You can visit me anytime.
أوقات ADVERB sometimes. بشتغل الأحد أوقات Sometimes I work on Sunday.

وقح ADJECTIVE (ELATIVE: أوقح)
rude. هيدي المرا كتير وقحة This woman is very rude.

وقع VERB (IMPERFECT: يوقع)
fall. الطفل وقع ع ركبتو The child fell on his knee.

وقّع VERB (IMPERFECT: يوقّع)
drop. التلميذ وقّع قلمو The student dropped his pen.

وقف VERB (IMPERFECT: يوقف)
stand. وقف جنب البيت He stood

near the house.
stand up وقفوا لما فاتت العروسة عالصالة. They stood up when the bride entered the hall.
stop وقفوا وتطلعوا ببعض. They stopped and looked at each other.

وقف VERB (IMPERFECT: يوقف)

stop وقف الموسيقى، ما عم بقدر إدرس هيك. Stop the music! I can't study like this.; وقف السيارة جنب البيت. He stopped the car near the house.

ولا DETERMINER

no, not any ليش ما في ولا كتاب بخزانة الكتب؟ Why aren't there any books in the bookcase?
none ولا واحد ولا واحد من المفاتيح مناسب للقفل. None of the keys fits the lock.

ولادة NOUN

birth ولادة طفلا الأول كان صعب. The birth of her first child was difficult.

ولد VERB (IMPERFECT: يولد)

be born البيبي ولد بالمستشفى. The baby was born at the hospital.

ولد NOUN (PLURAL: ولاد)

boy, child, kid الولد بيحضر تلفزيون بعد ما يخلص فرضو. The boy watches TV after he finishes his homework.
PLURAL NOUN ولاد **children, kids** كل ولادنا دكاترة. All of our children are doctors.

- While the singular noun refers to a boy (male), the plural can be a mixed group of boys and girls and can also refer to one's children (offspring), small or grown up.

ولّع VERB (IMPERFECT: يولّع)

light ولّع شمعة ليشوف بالعتمة. He lit a candle to see in the dark.

ويب سايت NOUN

website الشركة عندا ويب سايت. The company has a website.

ويك إند NOUN

weekend شو عامل بالويك إند؟ What are you doing on the weekend?

وين ADVERB

where وين عايش؟ Where do you live?

ي يـ ـيـ ـي

isolated
initial
medial
final

Yaa is the twenty-eighth and final letter of the Arabic alphabet. When it precedes a vowel, it is pronounced y (as in yes): يَ *ya,* يِ *yi,* يُ *yu,* يا *yē,* يو *yū.* It is also y in the diphthong: ـَيْ *ay* (as in n**igh**t). Otherwise, following a consonant, it is a long vowel: ـي *ē* (as in r**ai**n, but without the glide to y), as French **é** or German **eh**; ـي *ī* (as in **ea**t). At the end of a word, it is a short kasra sound (transcribed *i*) as in m**e**t, French è.

ا ب ت ث ج ح خ د ذ ر ز س ش ص ض ط ظ ع غ ف ق ك ل م ن ه و **ي**

ـي PRONOUN

my. هيدي بنتي. This is my daughter.
my own. عندي أوضتي. I have my own bedroom.

• **Pronoun suffixes** are used both as objects (on verbs) and possessive pronouns (on nouns). Only the first-person singular suffixes have separate forms for object and possessive. (➲ See table →)

يلي PRONOUN (ALSO: اللي)

that, who, which
هيدا الولد يلي ضرب البسينة! This is the boy who hit the cat!; ولعت الشموع يلي عالكيك. I lit the candles that are on the cake.

يمكن PSEUDO-VERB, INVARIABLE

(+ imperfect verb) **may, might** يمكن سافر الشهر الجاي. I might travel next month.

	WE	ME/MY
	نا	ـي¹ / ـني²
YOU(R) M.		ك
YOU PL.	كن	
YOU(R) F.		ك
HIM/HIS		ـه³ / ـه⁴
THEM/THEIR	ـن³ / ـين⁵ / ـهن⁶	
HER		ـا³ / ـيا⁵ / ـها⁶

¹ possessive; ² object; ³ after consonant; ⁴ after vowel; ⁵ after the vowel ي; ⁶ after other vowels

يمين NOUN (NO PLURAL) **right**
العربي ما بينكتب من الشمال لليمين. Arabic is not written from right to left.; لازم تلف عاليمين. You should turn right.

ADJECTIVE, INVARIABLE عندا جرح على إيدا اليمين. She has a cut on her right hand.

ـين

(dual suffix) **two** نقلت ع لبنان من سنتين. I moved to Lebanon two years ago.

- Note that two of something is expressed by this suffix in Levantine Arabic, instead of using a separate word for the number. See note for تنين.

يوم NOUN (PLURAL: إيام) **day** عدد إيام الأسبوع سبعة. The number of days in a week is seven. اليوم **today** عم بتعلم عربي اليوم. I'm learning Arabic today.

English-Arabic Index

This index is to help you locate Arabic entries in the dictionary. Keep in mind that words in English often have more than one meaning and are sometimes used as different parts of speech. For example, the English word 'age' can be a noun (how old one is) as well as a verb (to get older). If you look up a word in this index and are unfamiliar with the Arabic translations, you will need to look up each and examine its part of speech, usage in context (through the example sentences), and other grammatical information to find the right word and use it correctly. Although having a full English-Arabic side to the dictionary would be convenient, we have avoided this for two main reasons. It would mean repeating the same information several times in different places in the dictionary, tripling its size and doubling its cost. Also, there is value in taking time getting to know new words. If you quickly glance in the dictionary and find your answer, you are likely to forget that new information moments later. Finding Arabic words in the index, jotting them down or looping them on repeat in your short term memory while you look up their entries and then spending a few minutes studying the information there proves a much more effective learning tool. And this is the goal of a learner's dictionary.

ability قدرة

able: be able to • قادر • يقدر • قدر

about • تقريبا • بخصوص • عن • شي • حوالي • حوالي

above فوق

abroad برا

absolutely بالتأكيد

accelerate سرع

accident حادث

according to حسب

across عبر; across from مقابيل

act عمل حالو • فصل • مثل

active نشيط

activity نشاط

actor ممثل

actually بالحقيقة

additional إضافي

address عنوان

afraid خايف • خيفان

after that بعد هيك

after بعد • بعد ما

afternoon بعد الضهر

again عن جديد • مرة تانية

age ختير • عمر

agitated نفعل

ago من

agree وافق • قبل

air هوا

all كل

all right • أوكي • طيب • ماشي • ماشي حالو

allow خلى • سمح لـ

alone • لحالو • لوحدو • وحدو

along(side) حد

already من قبل

also	كمان
although	مع إنو • ولو إنو
always	دايما
am: I am	أنا
America	أميركا
amount; amount due	كمية ؛ حق
analysis	فحص
and; and so on	و ؛ ألخ
angry	معصب
animal	حيوان
another	تاني • غير
answer	جواب
ants	نمل
any	أي • حيلا
anyone	أي حدا • حيلا حدا • مين ما كان
anything	أي شي • حيلا شي • شو ما كان
anytime	أي وقت • حيلا وقت
anywhere	شي محل • شي مطرح • شي مكان
apartment	شقة
appear	بين
appearance	مظهر
appearing	مبين
apples	تفاح
appropriate	مناسب • ناسب
approximately	حوالي • شي
April	نيسان
Arabic; Levantine Arabic	عربي ؛ عربي شامي
area	مساحة • منطقة
arid	ناشف
arm	إيد
army	جيش
around	تقريبا • حوالي • حوالي • حول • شي
arrive (at)	وصل
art	فن
as; as well	كـ • لما • متل • متل ما • كمان
ask	سأل
assignment	فرض
at	بـ • عند
attack	هجم ع • هجوم
attempt	جرب • حاول
attention: pay attention	نتبه
August	آب
aunt	خالة • عمة
auntie	خالتو • عمتو
autumn	خريف
baby	بيبي • طفل
back	ضهر
bad	غلط • مش منيح
bag	جزدان • شنطة • كيس
bakery	فرن
ball	طابة
balloon	بالون
bananas	موز
bank	بنك • مصرف
basket	سلة
basketball	باسكت (بول)
bathe	تحمم
bathroom	تواليت • حمام
battle	حارب
bazaar	سوق
be; be ___ing	كان ؛ عم
beach	بحر • شط
beans	فاصوليا
bear	دب
beard	دقن • لحية
beautiful	حلو
because; because of	عشان • لأن ؛ بسبب • من

become صار	birth ولادة	bored زهِق
bed تخت	birthday عيد ميلاد;	boring ممِل
bedroom أوضة نوم •	birthday party حفلة	born ولد • خلق
غرفة نوم	العيد ميلاد	borrow ستعار
beer بيرة	bit: a little bit شوي =	both لتنين • تِنتات
before that قبل هيك	نتفة	bottle قنينة
before من • قبل ما • قبل	bite لقمة • كدشة	bottom كعب • أسفل
قبل	black أسود	bowl كاسة
begin بلش	blank فراغ	box علبة
beginning بداية	bleed نزف	boy ولد • صبي
behave تأدب • تصرف •	blind أعمى	branch فرع
عمل حالو	block سد • غطى	brave شجاع • جريء
behind ورا	blood دمّ	bread خبز; piece of
Beirut بيروت	blouse بلوزة	bread خبزة
believe صدّق • آمن	blow نفخ • ضربة • هب	breadth عرض
bell جرس	blue أزرق • محبط	break كسر • فرصة • فاصل
best أفضل • أزبط • أحسن	board تابلو • طلع • لوح	breakfast فطور • ترويقة;
• أول	boat شخطورة	have breakfast تروق
better أفضل • أزبط • أحسن	body جسم	breathe تنفّس
أفضل	boil غلى	bride عروسة
between بين • بينات	bone عضمة	bridge جسر
beverage مشروب	book كتاب • حجز	bright نضر
bicycle بيسيكليت	bookcase خزانة كتب	bring جاب
big كبير	bookstore مكتبة	brother خي
bike بيسيكليت	border طرف • حدود	brown بني
bird عصفور	bore زهِق	brush فرشي • فرشاية

مشط • مشط	car سيارة	chapter فصل
build بنى • عمر	card بطاقة • كارت	character طبيعة
building بناية	care about هتم بـ	charm سحر
built تعمر	careful تأنى • حذر • متأني • نتبه	chase طارد • لحق
burn حرق • حرق	careless مستلشق • مستهتر • مهمل	cheap رخيص
bus باص • بوسطة	carrots جزر	cheek خد
business شغل • مصلحة	carry حمل	cheese جبنة
busy مشغول	case حالة	chef طباخ
but بس	castle قصر	chicken دجاج
butter زبدة	cat بسة • بسينة	chickens دجاج
button كبسة	catch كمش • لقط	child طفل • ولد
buy شترى	cattle بقر	chocolate شوكولا
by عند; by means of بواسطة; by oneself لحالو • لوحدو • وحدو	cause تسبب بـ • خلى • سبب	choice إختيار • خيار
bye باي • مع السلامة	celebrity مشهور • نجم	choose ختار • نقى
café فرن • قهوة • كافيه	cell phone تلفون محمول • سيلولير • موبايل	church كنيسة
cake غاتو • كيك	center مركز	cinema سينما
calculate حسب	central مركزي	circle دائرة • دار
call تصل • تلفن • دق; phone call إتصال	century عصر • قرن	city مدينة
calm رايق	certain أكيد • كم • مأكد	class صف
camera كاميرا	chair كرسة	classroom صف
can تنكة • فيو • قادر • قدر	chance فرصة	classy راقي • كلاس
candle شمعة	change بدل • تغير • غير	clay معجون
cap شابو • طقية • كاسكيت		clean نضف • نضيف
		cleaning تنضيف
		clear صافي • واضح; clear up نقى

151 | Beginning Learner's Levantine Arabic Dictionary

clever ذكي	commercial تِجاري	correct صح • صحيح • صلح • مزبوط
climb تسلّق	common مألوف	correctness حقّ
clock ساعة	company شركة	cost تمن • حقّ • كلف
close سكر • قريب	compare قارن	couch كنباية
closet خزانة	complete خلص • كامل • كفّى • كمل	could كان فيو
cloth مفرش	computer كمبيوتر	count حسب • عدّ; count on تكل ع
clothes تياب	con غش	country بلد • وطن
clothing تياب	concern هم; show concern for هتم بـ	course مسار
cloud غيمة	condition شرط • وضع	courtyard ساحة
cloudy مغيم	contain حتوى ع	cousin قريب
clue دليل	content راضي	cover غطى
coat معطف • منطو	continent قارة	cows بقر
coffee قهوة	continue ستمر • كفّى	crackers مكسرات
coin عملة معدنية	control سيطر ع • سيطرة • ضبط	crash تحطم • صطدم
cold بارد • برد • بردان • برودة; make cold برد	controlling سيطرة	crazy مجنون
collect جمّع • لمّ	cook طبّاخ • طبخ	criminal حرامي
collection مجموعة	cookie بسكوتة • بيسكوي	cross قطع
college جامعة	cool بارد • برد • بردان	cry بكي
color لون • لوّن	coolness برد • برودة	cup فنجان
colored ملون	cop دركي • شرطي	cupboard خزانة
comb مشط • مشّط	copper نحاس	currency exchange صرف العملة
come back رجع • عاد	corn درة	custom عادة
come إجا • تاعا	corner زاوية • مفرق	cut جرح • قصّ • قطع
comfortable مريح		
coming جايي		

dad بابا • بي	dictionary قاموس	double دوبل • مزدوج
damage خرب	die مات	down محبط
dance رقص • رقصة	different مختلف	downstairs تحت
dangerous خطير	difficult صعب	draw رسم
dark عتمة • غامق	dining room غرفة سفرة	drawing رسمة
darling حبيب	dinner عشا; have dinner تعشى	dream حلم
date تاريخ		dress فستان
daughter بنت	direction إتجاه • جهة	dressed: get dressed لبس
day نهار • يوم	dirty وسخ	drink شرب • مشروب
dead ميت	discover كتشف	drive ساق
deceive خدع • غش	discussion نقاش	drop خفض • نزل • نقطة • وقع
December كانون الأول	disembark نزل	
decide قرر	dish صحن • طبق	drown غرق
decision قرار	dismiss زعب • طرد	dry ناشف
decline رفض	display عرض	dual مزدوج
decrease خفض • خفف • قلل • نخفض • نزل	disposition طبيعة	duck بطة
	distant بعيد	dust غبرة • نفض
deep عميق	distinctive مميز	duty مسؤولية • واجب
deer غزال	divide قسم	each كل; each other بعض
delicious طيب	do عمل	
department دائرة	doctor حكيم • دكتور	ear دينة
depend on عتمد ع	document مستند	early بكير
depressed محبط	dog كلب	earn قبض
desk طبقة • مكتب	doll لعبة	Earth الأرض
destroy خرب • دمر	dollar دولار	east شرق
develop تطور • نمى	door باب	

153 | Beginning Learner's Levantine Arabic Dictionary

easy سهل • هين	enemy عدو	evening هالمسا
eat أكل	engineering هندسة	event مناسبة
edge طرف	English إنكليزي	every كلّ
education تعليم • علم	enjoy نبسط بـ • ستمتع؛ enjoy oneself تسلى	everybody كل واحد
effect تأثير		everything كل شي
eggs بيض	enormous ضخم	everywhere كل محل • كل مطرح • كل مكان
Egypt مصر	enough كفى	
eight تمانة	enter دخل • فات	evidence دليل
eighteen تمنطعش	entertaining سلى	exactly بالظبط
eighty تمينين	entrance مدخل	exam(ination) إمتحان • فحص
either... or... أو... أو...	equal تساوى • قد بعض • متساوي	example: for example مثلا
electricity كهربا	equip زود	except إلا
elephant فيل	era عصر	excited محمّس • نفعل
elevate على	erase محى	exciting حماسي
eleven حدعش	eraser محاية	excuse me سوري • عفوا • لو سمحت • معليش
else تاني	escape هرب • هريبة	
email إيميل • رسالة إلكترونية	establish ثبّت	exercise تدرّب • تمرّن • تمرين • رياضة
	esteemed محترم	
emotion إحساس	et cetera ألخ	expect توقع
employee موظف	Europe أوروبا	expensive غالي
emptiness فراغ	even though مع إنو • ولو إنو	experience تجربة
empty (out) فضى		explain شرح
empty فاضي	even متساوي • مزوج	eye عين
enchantment سحر	evening مسا • in the evening المسا • this	façade واجهة
end آخر • خلص • نتهى • نهاية		face وج

fact حقيقة	feeling إحساس	fix ثبت • صلح
factory مصنع • معمل	female أنثى	fixed ثابت
fail فشل	fever حرارة	flag علم
fair صاحي • عادل	few: a few كم	flat مسطح
fall خريف • نخفض • نزل • وقع	fiancé خطيب	float عام
	fiancée خطيبة	flood فيضان
family عيلة	fifteen خمسطعش	floor أرض
famous مشهور	fifty خمسين	flour طحين
fancy راقي • كلاس	fight تخانق • تمشكل • حارب • قاتل • مشكل	flower وردة
far بعيد		fly دبان • طار
farewell: bid farewell ودع	figure عدد	fold طوى
	fill عبى • ملى	food أكل
farm مزرعة	film فيلم	fool خدع • ضحك ع • أخوت
fashion model عارضة أزياء • مودل أزياء	final أخير	
	finally أخيرا	foolish أخوت
fast سريع	find لقى	foot إجر
fat دهن • ناصح	fine ماشي حالو • منيح	for إلو • لـ • لعدة • مشان
father بي	finger أصبع	forbid منع
favorite مفضل	finish خلص	forbidden ممنوع
fear خاف من • خوف	fire حريق • زعب • طرد • قوس • نار	force جبر
fearful خايف		foreign(er) أجنبي
feathers ريش	first أول	forest غابة
February شباط	fish سمك	forget نسي
fed up زهق	fit ساع • ناسب	forgive سامح
feed طعمى	fitting لبق لـ • مطابق	fork شوكة
feel حس حالو	five خمسة	form شكل • شكل

155 | Beginning Learner's Levantine Arabic Dictionary

forty	أربعين
four	أربعة
fourteen	أربعطعش
fox	ثعلب
framework	هيكل
France	فرنسا
free	بلاش • حر • حرر; free time مجانا • مجاني وقت الفراغ
freedom	حرية
freeze	جلد • فرز
fresh	طازة
Friday	جمعة
friend	رفيق • رفيقة • صاحب • صاحبة
friendly	محب
frighten	خوف
from	من
front	واجهة; in front of قدام = بوج
fruit	فاكهة
full stop	نقطة
full	مليان
fun	تسلاية • سلى; have fun تسلى
funny	مهضوم
furniture	عفش • فرش
further	إضافي
future	مستقبل
gain	ربح
game	لعبة • مباراة
garbage	زبالة
garden	جنينة
gas(oline)	بنزين
gate	بوابة
general	شامل; in general بالإجمال
generality	إجمال
generally	بالإجمال
German	ألماني
get	جاب • حصل ع • طلع; get in/on وصل لـ; get out نزل; get up فاق
gift	هدية
girl	بنت
give	عطى
glad	مبسوط
glass	كباية
glasses	عوينات
go	راح; go around دار; go back رجع • عاد
out	ضهر
goat	عنزة
God	الله • رب
gold	دهب
good	منيح
goodbye	باي • مع; say goodbye السلامة; ودع
governor	حاكم
grade	علامة • نتيجة
graduate	تخرج
grandfather	جد
grandma	تيتا
grandmother	ست
grandpa	جدو
grass	عشب
grave	قبر
gray	رمادي
graze	رعى
Great Britain	بريطانيا
green	أخضر
greenery	زرع • نبات
ground	أرض
group	مجموعة
grow	كبر • نمى; grow old ختير

guest	ضيف • معزوم
guide	دل • ودّى
guitar	غيتار
gun	فرد
gym	دجم • نادي
habit	عادة
hair	شعر
half	نص
hall	صالة • قاعة
hammer	دق • مطرقة
hand	إيد
handwriting	خط
hang; hang up	سكر • علّق
hanging	معلّق
happen	صار
happiness	سعادة
happy	مبسوط
hard	صعب
hat	برنيطة
hate	كره
have; have to	عندو • إلو • ضروري • لازم
he	هو
head	راس
health	صحة
healthy	صحي
hear	سمع
heart	قلب
heat up	سخّن
heaven	الجنة
heavy	تقيل
height	طول
hello	مرحبا
help	ساعد • مساعدة
hens	دجاج
her	ـا
here	هون
hi	هاي
hide	تخبّى • خبّى
high	عالي
high-class	راقي • كلاس
hill	تلة
him	ـه • ـو
his	إلو • تبعو • ـه • ـو
history	تاريخ
hit	خبط • ضرب
hobby	هواية
hold	حمل • متلك • مسك
holiday	عيد
home	بيت
homework	فرض
honorable	شريف
hope	أمل • تمنى
horse	حصان
hospital	مستشفى
hot	سخن
hotel	أوتيل • فندق
hour	ساعة
house plant	زريعة
house	بيت
how; how much	كيف؛ قدي
huge	ضخم
hundred	مية • مئة
hung up	معلّق
hungry	جاع • جعان
hurry	ستعجل
hurt	جرح • وجع • وجّع
husband	جوز • زوج
I	أنا
ice	تلج
idea	فكرة
if	إذا • لو
ill	صاخن • مريض
illuminate	ضوّى
important	مهم
in	بـ • بعد
in order to	تـ • لـ

incident حادث	it هو ・ ه	killed نقتل
increase ارتفاع ・ رتفع ・ زاد ・ زيادة	Italian إيطالي	kind لطيف ・ منيح ・ نوع
	Italy إيطاليا	king ملك
inflate نفخ	itch رعى	kiss باس
information معلومة	its ه	kitchen مطبخ
injure جرح	jacket جاكيت	knee ركبة
insane مجنون	jam مربى	knife سكينة
inside بقلب	January كانون التاني	knock خبط ・ دق
instead of محلو ・ مطرحو ・ مكانو	jeans دجينز	know عرف
	job شغل ・ وظيفة	knowledge علم
intend قصد	join نضم لـ	label علم
interested in هتم بـ	joke مزحة	ladder سلم
interesting مشوق	Jordan الأردن	lady ست
internet: the internet الإنترنت	journalism صحافة	lamp لمبة
	journey رحلة ・ سفرة	land أرض ・ هبط
interview مقابلة	juice عصير	language لغة
into لـ	July تموز	large كبير
introduce طرح ・ عرض ・ عرف	jump نط	last آخر ・ أخير ・ ماضي; last night ليلة مبارح = مسا مبارح
	June حزيران	
inundated غرق	just بس ・ مجرد	
invent خترع	keep خلى; keep (doing) ستمر	late تأخر ・ مأخر
invite عزم		lately مؤخرا
invitee معزوم	key مفتاح	later بعدين
iron حديد ・ كوى	kid ولد	laugh ضحك; make laugh ضحك
island جزيرة	kids ولاد	
issue قصة ・ موضوع	kill قتل	law قانون

lazy كسول	ضوى	love حب ٠ حب
lead ترأس ٠ دل ٠ دليل ٠ ودى	like this هيك	low ضعيف ٠ واطي
leaf: leaves ورق شجر	like حب ٠ متل	lower خفض ٠ قلل ٠ وطى
learn تعلّم	line خط	luck حظ
leave ترك ٠ راح ٠ فل	lion أسد	lunch غدا; have lunch تغدى
Lebanese لبناني; Lebanese people = الشعب اللبناني اللبنانية	lip شفة	machine مكنة
	list لايحة ٠ ليستة	main رئيسي
	listen سمع	majority أكترية
	little صغير; a little شوي = نتفة; a little bit (of) شوية	make up تصالح
Lebanon لبنان		make خلي ٠ عمل
left شمال		male دكر
left-hand شمال	live عاش	man رجال
leg إجر	living room أوضة قعدة	many كتير
lend سلف ٠ عار	lock قفل ٠ قفل	map خريطة
length طول	lonely وحيد	margin طرف
less أقل	long ago زمان	mark علامة ٠ علم
lesson درس	long طويل; a long time ago من زمان	market سوق
let خلي ٠ سمح لـ		marriage زواج
letter حرف ٠ رسالة	look: look (at) تطلع; look (for) دور = فتش = نبش	married: get married تجوز ٠ تزوج
Levantine Arabic عربي شامي		marry تجوز ٠ تزوج
	looking مبين	marvel عجيبة
library مكتبة	looks مظهر	master رب
lie كذب ٠ كذبة	lord رب	match مباراة
life حياة	lose خسر ٠ ضيع	material مادة
lift رفع; lift up على	lot: a lot (of) كتير	
light ضو ٠ ولع; light up		

159 | Beginning Learner's Levantine Arabic Dictionary

matter	قصة • موضوع	miss	آنسة • شتاق لـ • فوت • مس	movie theater	سينما
May	أيار • يمكن	mistake	خطأ • غلطة	movie	فيلم
me	ـني	mister	سيد • مسيو	movies	سينما
meal	وجبة	mix	خلطة	Mr.	سيد • مسيو
mean	عنى • قصد	model	نموذج; fashion model • عارضة أزياء • مودل أزياء	Mrs.	ست • مدام
measure	قاس			much	كتير
measurement	قياس			museum	متحف
meat	لحمة	modern	عصري • مودرن	music	موسيقى
media	صحافة	mom	إم • ماما	must	لازم
medicine	دوا • طب	Monday	تنين	mustn't	لازم ما
meet	قابل • لتقى	money	مصاري	my	ـي
member	عضو	monkey	سعدان • قرد	nail	مسمار
memory	ذاكرة	month	شهر	name	إسم
mention	ذكر	moon	قمر	narrow	ضيق
merchandise	بضاعة	more	أكتر • كمان	nation	وطن
mere	مجرد	morning	صبح • in the morning • الصبح	nationality	جنسية
merely	بس			nature	طبيعة
message	رسالة	mosque	جامع	near	جنب
method	طريقة	most	أكترية • معظم	nearly	تقريبا
middle	نص • وسط	mother	إم	necessary	ضروري • لازم • مطلوب
might	يمكن	mountain	جبل		
milk	حليب	mouth	تم	neck	رقبة
million	مليون	move	تحرك • حرك • حركة • زاح • نقل	necklace	عقد
mind	عقل			necktie	ربطة
minute	دقيقة			need	بدو • حاجة • ضروري • لازم; in need of
misplace	ضيع	movement	حركة		

160 | Beginning Learner's Levantine Arabic Dictionary

بحاجة لـ	nose منخار	one's تبعو
needle إبرة	not ما • مش • منو	oneself حالو
neighbor جار	nothing ما شي	only بس
neighborhood حي	notice إنذار • لاحظ	open فتح • مفتوح
neither... nor... ...ولا ...لا	notify بلغ	opposite عكس • مقابيل
net شبك	November تشرين التاني	or أو
never mind معليش	now هلأ	orange ليمون
never أبدا	number رقم • عدد	order طلب • طلبية • وصى ع
new جديد	obey طاع	organize رتب • مرتب
news: the news الأخبار؛ piece of news خبر	object شي	other تاني • غير
newspaper جريدة	obligation واجب	our ـنا
next جاي؛ next to جنب • حد	obtain حصل ع	outer space فضا
nice حلو • لطيف • منيح	ocean محيط	outside برا
nickname دلع • لقب	October تشرين الأول	oven فرن
night ليل	of من	over عبر • فوق
nine تسعة	off مطفي	own خاص فيو
nineteen تسعتعش	offer عرض • قدم	page صفحة
ninety تسعين	office دائرة • مكتب	pain وجع
no لأ • ولا	often دايما	paint دهن • رسم
noble شريف	oil زيت	painting رسمة • لوحة
nobody ما حدا	okay أوكي • طيب • ماشي • ماشي حالو	pair جوز
noise صوت • ضجة	old ختيار • قديم	palace قصر
none ولا واحد	on ع • على	Palestinian فلسطيني
north شمال	once مرة	pants بنطالون
	one واحد	paper ورق؛ piece of

paper	ورقة
pardon	معليش • سوري
parents	أهل
park	صف • حديقة
parking lot	باركينغ • موقف
part	جزء
participate	شارك
partner	شريك
party	حفلة
pass	نجح • مرق • قضى
past	ماضي
path	ممر • مسار • طريق
pay; pay attention	دفع؛ نتبه
peace	سلام
pen	قلم
pencil	قلم رصاص
people	ناس • شعب
pepper	بهار
perfect	تمام
period	نقطة • فترة
person	شخص
pet	حيوان أليف
phone call	إتصال
phone line	خط
phone	تلفن • تصل • دق • تلفون
photo	صورة
photograph	صور • صورة
piano	بيانو
pick up	لم
pick	نقى • ختار
picnic	بيكنيك
picture; take a picture (of)	صورة • رسمة؛ صور
piece	قطعة • شقفة
pig	خنزير
pin	دبوس
pink	زهر
pita wrap	عروسة
pizza	بيتزا
place; in one's place =	مرتبة • محل • حط • مكان • مطرح؛ مطرحو = محلو = مكانو =
plane	طيارة
plant	زرع
plants	نبات • زرع
plastic	بلاستيك
plate	طبق • صحن
play	مسرحية • لعب
playing cards	ورق شدة
plaza	ساحة
please	بليز • إذا بتريد • من فضلك • عمول معروف • رضي
pleased	راضي
pocket	جيبة
point	نقطة
poison	سم
police	درك • بوليس • شرطة
police officer	دركي • بوليس • شرطي
police station	مركز الشرطة
polite	مهذب
pollute	لوث
polluted	ملوث
poor	فقير
popular	مشهور
portion	حصة
position	مركز • رتبة • منصب
possession	حوزة
possible	ممكن • معقول

potatoes بطاطا	pull شد ; سحب	ready جاهز ; make ready جهز = حضر
pour صب ; pour out كب	punish قاصص	
practice تمرن	pupil تلميذ • بوبو	real حقيقي
prepare جهز • حضر	pure صافي	reality حقيقة • in reality بالحقيقة
present حاضر • هدية	purple موف	
press صحافة • كبس	push دفش	really بالفعل • عنجد
pretty حلو	put حط ; put in order رتب ; put on لبس	receive جاب • وصل لـ
prevent منع		reconcile تصالح
previously من قبل	putty معجون	record سجل
price سعر	queen ملكة	red أحمر
prince أمير	question سؤال	refined راقي • كلاس
prison حبس	quick سريع	refrigerator براد
private خاص	quickly بسرعة	refuse رفض
prize جايزة	quiet رايق ; make quiet سكت	rely on تكل ع
probably الأرجح • ممكن		remember تذكر
problem مشكلة	quite بالفعل • كتير	remind ذكر
produce أنتج	rabbit أرنب	remove شال
product بضاعة • منتج	radiant نضر	rent أجار • ستأجر
profit ربح	radio راديو	repair صلح
promise وعد • وعد	rain شتت • شتي	repeat عاد • كرر
proper مناسب	rainy شتوي	reply رد
proposal عرض	raise ترقية • رفع • على	report بلغ • تشكى • تقرير • ربورتاج
protect حمى	rank رتبة • مرتبة • مركز	
provide زود	rather بس	require بدو
public شعب • عام • علني	reach حوزة • وصل	required ضروري • لازم • مطلوب
publish نشر	read قرا	

reserve	حجز	rock	حجرة • صخر • هز	say	قال
respected	شريف • محترم	role	دور	scare	خوف
response	رد	room	أوضة • غرفة	scene	مشهد
responsibility	مسؤولية	rope	حبلة	school	مدرسة
rest	راحة • رتاح	round	مدور	science	علم
restaurant	مطعم	route	طريق	scissors	مقص
restroom	تواليت • حمام	rubber	مطاط	score	علامة
result	نتج • نتيجة	rude	وقح	search	دور • فتش • نبش
retail	تجاري	rule	حكم • قاعدة • قانون	seaside	بحر
return	رجع • رجعة • عاد • عودة	ruler	حاكم • مسطرة	season	فصل
rice	رز	run	ركض	seat	مقعد
rich	غني	rush	ستعجل	second	تاني
ride	ركب	sad	حزين • زعل • زعلان	section	فصل
right	حق • صحيح • مزبوط • معو حق • يمين	safe	آمن • خزنة	see	شاف
		safety	سلامة	seem	بين
		sail	أبحر • شراع	select	ختار • نقى
right-hand	يمين	salt	ملح	selection	خيار
rightness	حق	same: the same __	ذات نفس الـ = الـ	sell	باع
ring	خاتم • رن			send	بعت
		sample	نموذج	sentence	جملة • حكم • حكم
rise	إرتفاع • رتفع • زاد • شرق	sand	رمل		
		sandwich	ساندويشة	September	أيلول
river	نهر	satisfy	رضي	serve	خدم • ضيف
road	طريق	Saturday	سبت	set free	حرر
roam	كزدر	Saudi Arabia	السعدية	set	حط
rob	سرق	save	خلص • سجل • وفر	seven	سبعة

164 | Beginning Learner's Levantine Arabic Dictionary

سبعتعش seventeen	عيط shout	ستين sixty
سبعين seventy	عرض • فرجى show	قياس size
كذا several	تحمم shower	موهبة skill
جنس • سيكس sex	سكر shut	بشرة • جلد skin
ظل • ظلل • في shade	صاخن • مريض ; get sick مرض	تنورة skirt
خيال shadow	جنب • جهة • طرف • side ميلة	سما sky
خض • رجف • هز shake	رمز • علامة sign	نام • نوم sleep
شكل • شكل shape	أشار • إرسال signal	شقفة • قطعة slice
حصة share	سكت • سكوت silence	بطيء ; slow down بطأ • خفف slow
حاد • ذكي sharp	أهبل • سخيف • غبي silly	شوي شوي • ع مهلو slowly
هي she	فضة silver	صغير small
خروف sheep	هين simple	ريحة • شم smell
sheet: sheet of paper ورقة	إلو... ما • صارلو... ما • من since	بتسم • بسمة smile
رف shelf	غنى sing	دخان • دخن smoke
لمع shine	أعزب • إنفرادي • واحد single	تدخين smoking
سفينة ship	مغسلة sink	تلج snow
قميص shirt	إستاذ sir	عشان هيك • ف • فإذا • so كتير • كرمال هيك • مشان هيك; so that ت • لـ
جزمة • صباط shoes	إخت sister	صابون soap
قوص shoot	قعد sit	فوتبول soccer
تسوق • محل shop	وضع situation	إجتماعي social
شوبينغ; go shopping تسوق	ستة six	فردة كلسات sock
قصير short	سطعش sixteen	كلسات socks
لازم should		كنباية sofa
كتف shoulder		

soft رايق • طري	spell هجّى	stop خلص • محطة • وقّف • وقف
some شي • كم	spend صرف • قضّى	store خزن • محل
somebody حدا	spill كبّ	storm عاصفة
someone حدا	spoon ملعقة	story قصة
something شي	sport رياضة • سبور	strange غريب
sometimes أوقات	spread نشر • دهن; spread out منتشر	street شارع
somewhere شي محل • شي مطرح • شي مكان	spring ربيع	strike ضربة
son إبن	square ساحة • مربع	strong قوي
song غنية	stable ثابت	structure هيكل
soon قريبا	stake حصة	student تلميذ
sorry سوري • عفوا • I'm sorry معليش • بعتذر	stamp ختم • طابع	studies دراسة
	stand (up) وقف	study درس
sort نوع	star مشهور • نجم • نجمة	studying دراسة
sound صوت	start بلش	stupid أهبل • غبي
soup شوربة	state وضع	subject مادة • موضوع
south جنوب	station محطة	substance مادة
space مساحة • outer space فضا	stay بقي • ضلّ	subway مترو
	steal سرق	success نجاح
speak حكي • قال لـ	steam بخار	successful ناجح
special مميز; special occasion مناسبة	step خطوة • درجة • دعس	sudden مفاجئ
	stiff جامد	sugar سكر
speech حكي • خطاب	still بعد	suit لبق لـ
speed سرعة; speed up سرع	stipulation شرط	suitable مطابق • مناسب • ناسب
	stomach بطن	
	stone حجرة • صخر	summer صيف • صيفية

166 | Beginning Learner's Levantine Arabic Dictionary

sun	شمس	tall	طويل	is/are	في
Sunday	أحد	taste	داق	therefore	عشان هيك • ف • فإذا • كرمال هيك • مشان هيك
sunny	مشمس	taxi	تاكسي		
supermarket	سوبر ماركت	tea	شاي	these	هال • هول
supply	زود	teach	علم	they	هن
support	مساعدة	teacher	إستاذ • معلمة	thick	سميك
sure	أكيد	team	فريق	thief	حرامي
surprise	فاجأ	tears	دمع	thin	رفيع
sweet	حلو	telephone	تلفون	thing	شغلة • شي
swim	تسبح • سبح	television	تلفزيون	think	فكر
swimming pool	بيسين • مسبح	tell	قال لـ	third	تالت
		temperature	حرارة	thirteen	تلتطعش
sword	سيف	ten	عشرة	thirty	تلاتين
symbol	رمز • علامة	tennis	تنس	this	هال • هيدا • هيدي
Syria	سوريا	terrible	رهيب	those	هوليك
Syrian	سوري	test	فحص • إمتحان	though	ولو إنو
table	طاولة	than	من	thousand	ألف
tail	دنب	thank you	شكرا • مرسي	threat	تهديد
take off	شال	thanks	شكرا • مرسي	three	تلاتة
take part	شارك	that	إنو • اللي • هيداك • هيديك • يلي	throw away	كب
take	أخد			throw	رمى
tale	قصة	the	الـ	Thursday	خميس
talent	موهبة	their	ـن	thus	هيك
talk	حكي	them	ـن	ticket	بطاقة • تيكت
talking	حكي	then	بعدين	tidy up	رتب
		there	هونيك ; there		

167 | Beginning Learner's Levantine Arabic Dictionary

tidy	مرتّب	train	ترين	unit	وحدة
tie	ربط	tranquil	رايق	university	جامعة
tight	ضيق	trash	زبالة	unmarried	أعزب
time	وقت • مرة	travel	سافر	until	لـ • لحد • لحد ما
tire	دولاب	trees	شجر	unwell	مريض • صاخن
tired	تعبان	trip	رحلة • سفرة	up	فوق
title	عنوان	trouble	مشكلة	upset	زعلان; get upset زعل
to	لـ • على • ع • ت	trousers	بنطالون	upstairs	فوق
today	اليوم	trust	وثق • ثقة	us	ـنا
toe	أصبع إجر	try	حاول • جرب	use	ستعمل
together	مع بعض • سوا	T-shirt	تي شيرت	useful	مفيد
tomatoes	بندورة	Tuesday	تلاتة	usual: as usual	متل العادة
tomorrow	بكرا; the day after tomorrow بعد بكرا	turn	لف • دور • برم; turn down وطى; turn on ضوى; turn off طفى	usually	بالعادة
tonight	الليلة	turned off	مطفي	vacation	فرصة • عطلة
too (also)	كمان	TV	تي في • تلفزيون	value	تمن
tool	أداة	twelve	طنعش	vegetables	خضرة
tooth	سن	twenty	عشرين	very	كتير; very much كتير
top	أول	twice	مرتين	via	بواسطة
topic	موضوع	two	ـين • تنين	view	منظر • مطل
total	مجموع	type	نوع • كتب	village	ضيعة
touch	سطع • دقر	uncle	عم • خال	visit	زيارة • زار
toward	تجاه	under	تحت	visitor	زاير
town	بلدة	underside	أسفل	voice	صوت
toy	لعبة	understand	فهم		

168 | Beginning Learner's Levantine Arabic Dictionary

volume صوت	wedding عرس	مرة = مدامة
wait نطر • نطرة	Wednesday إربعا	wild بري
waiter غارسون	week أسبوع • جمعة	will رح • لح
waitress غارسونة	weekend إند عطلة • ويك	win ربح
wake up فاق • فيق • وعى	weigh زان	wind هوا
walk مشي	weight وزن	window شباك
wall حيط	welcome أهلا • ستضاف	wine نبيد
want to بدو	well بير • منيح	winter شتوية
want بدو	west غرب	wire سلك
war حرب	wet رطب	wise عاقل
wardrobe خزانة	what شو	wish أمنية • تمنى
warm دافي; warm up سخن	whatever أي شي • شو ما كان	with مع
warning إنذار	wheel دولاب	without بدون • بلا
wash غسل	when أيمتى • بس • لما	woman مرا
waste زبالة • ضيع	where وين	wonder تعجب • عجبية
watch حضر • ساعة	which أيا • اللي • يلي	word كلمة
water مي	while بينما • وعم	work شتغل • شغل
way طريق • طريقة	white أبيض	working ماشي
we نحنا	who اللي • مين • يلي	world عالم
weak ضعيف	whoever مين ما كان	worry هم
wear لبس	why ليه	worse أسوأ • أضرب
wearing لابس	wide واسع	worst أسوأ • أضرب
weather طقس	widespread منتشر	wound جرح
website موقع إلكتروني • ويب سايت	width عرض	write كتب
	wife زوجة; wife (of)	written نكتب
		wrong الحق عليه • غلط

169 | Beginning Learner's Levantine Arabic Dictionary

yard ساحة
year سنة
yell عيّط
yellow أصفر; turn yellow صفرّ

yes أي
yesterday مْبارح;
   yesterday evening مسا مبارح
yet بعد
you إنت • إنتو • إنتي • ـك

ـك • ـكن
young صغير
your ـك • ـكـ • ـكن
zero صفر
zoo حديقة حيوانات

lingualism

Visit our website for information on current and upcoming titles, free excerpts, and language learning resources.

www.lingualism.com

Printed in Great Britain
by Amazon